THE NEW YORK
YANKEES HOME RUN
ALMANAC

THE BRONX BOMBERS' MOST HISTORIC, UNUSUAL, AND TITANIC DINGERS

BY DOUGLAS B. LYONS

FOREWORD BY MARTY APPEL

SPORTS
PUBLISHING

Sports Publishing books may be purchased in bulk at special discounts for sales promotion, corporate gifts, fund-raising, or educational purposes. Special editions can also be created to specifications. For details, contact the Special Sales Department, Sports Publishing, 307 West 36th Street, 11th Floor, New York, NY 10018 or sportspubbooks@skyhorsepublishing.com.

Sports Publishing® is a registered trademark of Skyhorse Publishing, Inc.®, a Delaware corporation.

Visit our website at www.sportspubbooks.com.

10 9 8 7 6 5 4 3 2 1

Library of Congress Cataloging-in-Publication Data

Names: Lyons, Douglas B., author.
Title: The New York Yankees home run almanac : the Bronx bombers'
 most historic, unusual, and titanic dingers / Douglas B. Lyons.
Description: New York, NY : Sports Publishing, 2018. | Includes index.
Identifiers: LCCN 2018005209 | ISBN 9781683581956 (alk. paper)
Subjects: LCSH: New York Yankees (Baseball team)--History. | Home runs
 (Baseball)
Classification: LCC GV875.N4 L96 2018 | DDC 796.357/64097471--dc23
LC record available at https://lccn.loc.gov/2018005209

Cover design by Tom Lau
Cover photo credit Associated Press

ISBN: 978-1-68358-195-6
Ebook ISBN: 978-1-68358-196-3

Printed in the United States of America

DEDICATION

This book is dedicated to the late David Vincent. David has forgotten more statistics, stories, and lore about home runs than I will ever know. Wait—that's not completely true. David never forgot *anything*!

Want to know who hit the most home runs on his birthday—or on *your* birthday?[1] David could tell you. Want to know which lefty hit the most home runs at Sicks Stadium?[2] David knew.

I have written/cowritten five books of baseball history and trivia. Every time I was unable to find the answer to a home run question such as "Who hit the most home runs on a Thursday?"[3] David was able to provide the answer in about three minutes. Not only did David answer my questions, he provided answers to questions that I hadn't yet asked, e.g., "Who hit the most home runs on a *Wednesday*?"

One day outside Fenway Park, I had the pleasure of introducing David to my brother Jeffrey—two of the most devout Red Sox fans I know.

How much did David know about the game? He had a full-time job, but he made time to be the official scorer for the Washington Nationals. In addition to his expertise on home

---

1. I do.
2. Home of the Seattle Pilots, 1969.
3. How would you look that up?

runs, he was an expert on all things umpire-related, ejections, and players batting out of turn.

David was the author of *Home Run's Most Wanted: The Top 10 Book of Monumental Dingers, Prodigious Swingers, and Everything Long-Ball.* David won numerous awards from the Society of American Baseball Research.

David was also a consultant on home run statistics and history to a number of major-league teams. I'm very proud to have called him my friend.

After a brave battle with cancer, David passed away on July 2, 2017. I will miss him greatly.

TABLE OF CONTENTS

FOREWORD
BY MARTY APPEL

Doug Lyons is right when he says that you think of home runs when you think of the New York Yankees.

The great 1961 Yankees, the team of Roger Maris and Mickey Mantle chasing Babe Ruth's record and six players topping 20 homers, hit 240 as a team, a major-league record. Much was made of that at the time, along with the accolades paid to Maris himself, who had 61.

But here is a remarkable oddity: The Bronx Bombers then went 46 seasons—almost half a century!—before leading the league again. Not until 2007 did they manage to top that chart. (They tied in 2004.)

The laws of probability cry out on this one. It wasn't as if they had abandoned their playbook and become a running team. After all, they still packed power. But it just was.

I suspect you had no idea about this improbable stat, largely because little or no attention is given to which team hits the most home runs each year. The fact that the Yankees could go so long without leading the league—and still be thought of as the team of home run hitters, playing in inviting Yankee Stadium—is remarkable.

Also remarkable is the effort Doug has made in compiling these milestone home runs in this volume. Some are memorable, some are forgotten, but they do help to reinforce the belief that the Yankees are where you turn when you want to play some long ball.

The mere roll call of sluggers over the years who have worn that uniform and socked those baseballs bring awe to fans.

Think of this: the franchise has recorded over 15,500 home runs since it began, but 5,842—or nearly 40 percent— have been hit by just their top 20 all-time home run hitters.

Babe Ruth, Mickey Mantle, Lou Gehrig, Joe DiMaggio, Yogi Berra, Alex Rodriguez, Bernie Williams, Jorge Posada, Derek Jeter, Graig Nettles, Don Mattingly, Jason Giambi, Mark Teixeira, Dave Winfield, Robinson Cano, Roger Maris, Bill Dickey, Tino Martinez, Paul O'Neill, and Charlie Keller.

Take a bow guys.

(Did we say Derek Jeter? Somehow one seldom thought of him hitting one out when he came to bat, but there he sits at number nine all-time with 260. And, he is second all-time in postseason home runs).

The story begins, of course (after a forgettable first 17 years), with the Mighty Bambino, that Sultan of Swat, the great George Herman "Babe" Ruth.

He joined the Yankees in their 18th season. They shared the Polo Grounds with the New York Giants, and Ruth exploded onto the scene with 54 home runs at a time when the "Dead Ball Era" was probably still in place, if not fading away. After all, led by Ruth, the Yankees hit 115 homers that year. The other seven teams hit just 254, an average of 36 each. So if there was a lively ball in 1920 when Ruth hit his 54, where was everyone else?

(I have my own suspicion: a livelier ball was being ushered in, but cost-conscious owners were not about to discard leftover dead balls. Nothing was discarded in those days. Games were probably played with a mix of both.)

The Polo Grounds was remarkably inviting with very short foul lines. Ruth later said that he preferred hitting there to Yankee Stadium, the very "House That Ruth Built!"

And now, we should indeed talk about Yankee Stadium.

A lot of the events in this book happened when the Yankees played at Hilltop Park, the Polo Grounds, or Shea Stadium—or happened on the road, or were the work of opposing players on the road. But it is hard to talk Yankees or home runs without turning our eyes to the majesty of Yankee Stadium, whose architectural grandeur seemed designed to capture the beauty of the game that is inherent in the home run. It seemed designed to celebrate the drama of a home run blast.

"It was like pitching in the Grand Canyon," noted Sandy Koufax at the 1963 World Series.

Ruth never hit one into the upper deck at Yankee Stadium. The original stadium had the bleachers running foul pole to foul pole. After the 1926 season, the mezzanine and upper decks were extended into fair territory in left field, but a matching move in right field did not occur until after Ruth left the Yankees in 1934. His homers still had the high arc that was a product of his swing that gave the fans plenty of time to ooh and aah as they followed the trajectory. So even without an inviting upper deck, there was majesty in his home runs. Every fan I spoke to who saw him play would describe it the same way—with the result matching the expectation. He was just a joy to behold, a showman whose stage was grass and dirt.

Of course every fan I spoke to from that era "was there the day Babe homered," and I used to think that seemed just a little improbable, although I wasn't about to deny them the sweet memory. But when you think about it, he did hit one just about every three games, so one's chances of seeing one were awfully good, especially if you were at a doubleheader. And for an opposing team to face the Yankees in a three- or four-game series meant almost for sure that Babe was going to unload at least once.

As this is being written, a Yankees rookie named Aaron Judge has electrified New York by breaking Joe DiMaggio's franchise rookie record of 29. On this team, when you start picking off brand names like DiMaggio, heads turn. We know not what the future holds for this player; things happen. But for now, he has everyone pairing "Yankees" and "home run" again. Will he become an immortal? Or the latest version of Kevin Maas or Shane Spencer? That's baseball, folks. That's why they play the games.

I was in the right field stands when the last game at the "old stadium" was played in 2008. José Molina hit the last home run there (Ruth had hit the first). But in the ninth inning, I remember thinking, *Okay guys, last chance—no one has ever hit a fair ball out of this place.*

It didn't happen, and as this is written, no one has accomplished the feat in the new place either. Some standards may have to be in place forever. Or Doug Lyons may have to hurry up with an updated edition.

PREVIOUS BOOKS
BY DOUGLAS B. LYONS

The Baseball Geek's Bible: All the Facts and Stats You'll Ever Need

Baseball: A Geek's Guide

American History: A Geek's Guide

100 Years of Who's Who in Baseball

With Jeffrey Lyons

Out of Left Field: Over 1,134 Newly Discovered Amazing Baseball Records, Connections, Coincidences, and More!

Curveballs and Screwballs: Over 1,286 Incredible Baseball Facts, Finds, Flukes, and More!

Short Hops and Foul Tips: 1,734 Wild and Wacky Baseball Facts

With Joe Castiglione

Broadcast Rites and Sites: I Saw It on the Radio with the Boston Red Sox

Can You Believe It?

With Eddie Feigner and Anne Marie Feigner
From an Orphan to a King

With Jim Leyritz and Jeffrey Lyons
Catching Heat: The Jim Leyritz Story

PREFACE

As of 2017, there are thirty Major League Baseball teams. But if you ask any fan—serious or casual—which team is most associated with the phrase "home run," I believe the overwhelming majority would answer, "The New York Yankees." They don't call them the "Bronx Bombers" for nothing.

Babe Ruth did not invent the home run, but he popularized it and made it seem less vulgar. A Ruthian blast was a sight to behold. It changed the entire complexion of the game. Sure, a successful bunt is exciting. So is a great catch, a pick-off, a hidden-ball trick, or a stolen base. Exciting, yes. But not *electrifying* like a 400-foot blast into the upper deck or out of the park entirely by Ruth, Lou Gehrig, Mickey Mantle, Reggie Jackson, Alex Rodriguez, Whitey Ford [!], or Aaron Judge. Even an inside-the-park grand slam by pitcher Mel Stottlemyre evokes this kind of excitement. There is nothing like it.

Here, then, is a month-by-month recounting of historic, important, unusual, or titanic home runs, hit mostly by Yankees. Statistics are accurate through the end of the 2017 baseball season.

ACKNOWLEDGMENTS

This book could not have been written without Retrosheet.org and Baseball-reference.com,—the researcher's best friends. Also, my thanks to David Vincent—*the* expert on all things home-run-related—Marty Appel, Jim Kaat, John Flaherty, Tony Morante of the New York Yankees, Dan Schlossberg, and Matt Rothenberg at the National Baseball Hall of Fame.

A special thank you to John Horne Jr., coordinator of rights & reproductions at the National Baseball Hall of Fame Library.

A Note on Photographs

I spent hours at New York City's massive 42nd Street Library poring over microfilms, trying to find newspaper photographs of the home runs mentioned in this book. Sad to say, newspaper photographs of many of them do not exist.

All photographs in this book are from the wonderful collection of the National Baseball Hall of Fame and Museum in Cooperstown, New York, except where noted.

INTRODUCTION
BY DOUGLAS B. LYONS

One of the things that I love about baseball is how many memorable moments there are in the game. While many of baseball's memorable moments do *not* involve who hit a home run, who scored, or who won the game, this book isn't about those moments.

It's about home runs—dingers, round-trippers, four-baggers, and mighty clouts—specifically home runs involving the New York Yankees. Most were hit *by* Yankees, but I have included many that were hit *against* the Yankees.

Trying to pick *the* greatest, *the* most important, most historic, or most memorable Yankees home run is a pointless task. There are too many to choose from. It's like trying to select your favorite child.

Among those worthy of consideration (in chronological order) are:

- The first Yankees home run, hit by Jeff Sweeney on May 5, 1913.
- Casey Stengel's inside-the-park home run for the New York Giants on October 10, 1923, in the first World Series game at brand new Yankee Stadium.
- Babe Ruth's 3 home runs in one World Series game, October 6, 1926.

- Babe Ruth's 60th home run of the season, September 30, 1927.
- Babe Ruth's 3 home runs in one World Series game—for the *second* time—October 9, 1928.
- Lou Gehrig's 4 home runs in one game, June 3, 1932.
- Babe Ruth's October 1, 1932, "Called Shot" in Game Three of the World Series.
- Mickey Mantle's titanic blast off Chuck Stobbs on April 17, 1953—said to be the first tape-measure home run.
- Bill Mazeroski's homer against the Yankees on October 13, 1960, in the bottom of the ninth inning of Game Seven of the World Series to win the game and the series for the Pittsburgh Pirates.
- October 1, 1961—Roger Maris's 61st home run of the season.
- Mickey Mantle's record 18th World Series home run, October 15, 1964.
- Mel Stottlemyre's inside-the-park grand slam on July 20, 1965.
- Chris Chambliss's walk-off home run on October 14, 1976, in the bottom of the ninth inning of the deciding Game Five of the American League Championship Series to send the Yankees to the World Series.
- Reggie Jackson's 3 home runs in Game Six of the World Series, October 18, 1977.
- The "Bucky Dent Home Run" on October 2, 1978, during the Yankees–Red Sox playoff to determine the winner of the American League East.
- George Brett's "Pine Tar" home run against the Yankees on July 24, 1983.
- Jim Leyritz's 3-run home run on October 23, 1996, in Game Four of the World Series.

- Jim Leyritz's home run at Yankee Stadium on October 27, 1999—the last of the twentieth century.
- Derek Jeter's November 1, 2001, home run in Game Four of the World Series.
- Hideki Matsui's grand slam in his very first Yankee Stadium game on April 8, 2003.
- Aaron Boone's walk-off home run in Game Seven of the American League Championship Series on October 16, 2003, to send the Yankees to the World Series.

These and the many other home runs in this book only took an instant to hit, but they provide memories, debates, and discussions that will last a lifetime.

JANUARY

DID YOU KNOW?

The most home runs hit by one team against another in a single season is 48, hit by the 1956 New York Yankees against the Kansas City Athletics.

January 3, 1920

The New York Yankees Purchase Babe Ruth from the Boston Red Sox

The New York Yankees purchased the contract of George Herman "Babe" Ruth from the Boston Red Sox for $125,000[em dash]an enormous sum at the time, the highest purchase price to that point. While the purchase of Ruth *made* the Yankees (he led them to seven American League pennants and four World Championships), it broke the heart of Bostonians and all New Englanders. In 1919, his last season in Boston, when he pitched in 17 games, Ruth hit 29 home runs, the most in the majors. In 1920, his first in New York, he smashed 54, again leading both leagues. What followed was "The Curse of the Bambino": The Boston Red Sox did not win a World Series for 85 years, between 1919 and 2003.

January 3, 1973

George M. Steinbrenner III Buys the New York Yankees

Tampa, Florida shipbuilder George M. Steinbrenner III— "The Boss"—bought the New York Yankees from CBS. He promised to be a "hands-off"[4] owner.

Steinbrenner owned the Yankees for 38 years, 1973– 2010—longer than anyone else. During that time, the team hit over 6,500 home runs and led the American League in home runs three times: 2004, 2007, and 2009.

---

4. Ha!

January 5, 1993

Reg-Gie in the Hall of Fame

Reginald Martinez "Reggie" Jackson, "the straw that stirs the drink," was elected to the National Baseball Hall of Fame. During his five years (1977–1981) with the New York Yankees, he clobbered 144 home runs and earned the nickname "Mr. October." Jackson's career batting average of just .262 is the lowest for any outfielder in Cooperstown.

January 9, 1960

"Home Run Derby"

The first episode of the half-hour black-and-white TV show *Home Run Derby*, hosted by Mark Scott, was aired. This episode pitted Willie Mays of the San Francisco Giants against Mickey Mantle of the New York Yankees. Mantle won $2,000.[5]

The show was filmed at Wrigley Field, home of the Los Angeles Angels of the Pacific Coast League.

January 11, 1915

Jacob Ruppert and Tillinghast L. Huston Buy the Yankees

Bill Devery and Frank Farrell sold the Yankees to Jacob Ruppert and Tillinghast L. Huston for $460,000. The 1914 Yankees hit a total of 12 home runs. Roger Peckinpaugh hit the most (3).

---

5.   Mantle's 1960 salary from the Yankees was said to be $60,000.

January 12, 1934

Babe Ruth Accepts a Salary Cut
from the New York Yankees

In 1933, when he hit 34 home runs, New York Yankees slugger Babe Ruth was paid $52,000. But he took a $17,000 salary cut to play in 1934 for only $35,000—still the highest salary in the majors, but Ruth, then thirty-nine, was nearing the end of his career.

January 13, 2005

The North Dakota House of Representatives
Wants Roger Maris in the Hall of Fame

On October 1, 1961, Roger Maris of the New York Yankees hit his 61st home run of the year, breaking Babe Ruth's record of 60, which had stood since 1927. Although Maris was born in Hibbing, Minnesota, he moved to Fargo, North Dakota, and

Roger Maris

made it his home. On this date, the North Dakota House of Representatives passed resolution number 3006 calling for Maris's election to the Baseball Hall of Fame. A copy of the resolution was sent to all members of the Hall's Veterans Committee.[6]

January 14, 1954

Joe DiMaggio Marries Marilyn Monroe

Former New York Yankees slugger Joe DiMaggio married Marilyn Monroe at City Hall in San Francisco. Unfortunately, the marriage lasted only 274 days. They were divorced in October of that year.

January 15, 1958

The New York Yankees Are on the Air!

The New York Yankees announced that they would broadcast 140 games in 1958, including 63 road games, on WPIX-TV. The Bronx Bombers hit 164 home runs in 1958, the most in the American League.

January 16, 1974

Mickey Mantle and Whitey Ford are Elected to the Baseball Hall of Fame

Mickey Mantle (536 home runs) and Edward Charles "Whitey" Ford (228 home runs surrendered, 3 home runs hit),

6. Maris is so revered in North Dakota that he was given the state's highest honor, the Theodore Roosevelt Rough Rider Award, on January 4, 1964. Fewer than 50 people (including Lawrence Welk, Peggy Lee, Secretary of State Warren Christopher, Angie Dickenson, and Bobby Vee) have had this honor bestowed on them.

Yankees teammates from 1953 to 1967, were both elected to the Baseball Hall of Fame.

January 22, 1913

Yankees and Giants to Share the Polo Grounds

The New York Giants of the National League agreed to rent their home ballpark, the Polo Grounds in Manhattan, to the newly named American League New York Yankees.

The Yankees remained at the Polo Grounds, where they hit a total of 336 homers (including 4 from the 1921 and 1922 World Series), until they started outdrawing the Giants and moved to Yankee Stadium in 1923.

FEBRUARY

You've got to be doing something right to spend 14 years as a catcher in the major leagues. John Flaherty, a native of New York City, was inducted into the George Washington University Athletic Hall of Fame for his baseball prowess and then was a big-league catcher for the Red Sox, Tigers, Padres, Devil Rays, and Yankees from 1992 to 2005. During that time, he hit 80 home runs and had a 27-game hitting streak.

Not all of his home runs were hit in the United States.

On May 29, 1995, while playing for the Detroit Tigers, Flaherty homered at SkyDome in Toronto, Ontario, Canada. The blast came in the ninth inning off Darren Hall of the Blue Jays with one out and Bobby Higginson on base.

When the Padres played in Monterrey, Mexico, on August 16, 1996, Flaherty homered off Robert Person of the New York Mets.

But when the Yankees opened the 2004 season against the Tampa Bay Devil Rays in Tokyo on March 30 and 31, Jorge Posada caught every inning of both games—denying Flaherty the opportunity to become the first player to homer in four countries.

February 4, 2010

The Ball That Alex Rodriguez Smashed for His 500th Home Run Is Sold at Auction

The ball that Alex Rodriguez of the New York Yankees hit for his 500th career home run on August 4, 2007, was sold at auction to an anonymous buyer for $103,579.

February 6, 1895

Babe Ruth Is Born

George Herman "Babe" Ruth, who hit 714 major-league home runs—659 for the Yankees—was born in Baltimore, Maryland.

February 6, 1921

The New York Yankees Buy Land in the Bronx for a New Stadium

The New York Yankees announced the purchase for $675,000 of 10 acres in the Bronx on which they would erect a new stadium—Yankee Stadium, directly across the Harlem River from their former home, the Polo Grounds, where they were tenants of the New York Giants. The new structure went up in less than a year.

February 7, 1949

Joe DiMaggio Signs the First $100,000-a-Year Contract

On February 7, 1949, Joe DiMaggio signed a one-year contract with the New York Yankees for $100,000 for the 1949 season—making him the first American League player to earn over $99,000.

That season, the thirty-four-year-old DiMaggio hit 14 home runs and batted .346.

February 9, 2001

Derek Jeter Signs a $189 Million, 10-Year Contract with the Yankees

Although not known primarily as a home run hitter (20 years, 260 career homers, including 1 grand slam), Derek Jeter was certainly the face of the New York Yankees. The 10-year contract he signed, for $189 million, made him the second highest-paid baseball player ever—behind Alex Rodriguez's 10-year, $252 million contract.

February 9, 2009

Alex Rodriguez Admits Using Performance-Enhancing Drugs Before He Came to the Yankees

After years of denials, New York Yankees third baseman Alex Rodriguez, who hit 351 home runs for the Yankees from 2004 to 2016, admitted to having used performance-enhancing drugs between 2001 and 2003 while he was with the Texas Rangers.

February 14, 1913

Mel Allen Is Born

Mel Allen (born Melvin Israel), the "Voice of the Yankees" (1939 to 1964), was born in Birmingham, Alabama. Allen's memorable home run call was "It's going, going, *gone!*" During his tenure, he called most of the Yankees' home runs.

February 17, 1943

You're in the Army Now, Joe DiMaggio!

Twenty-seven-year-old Joe DiMaggio enlisted in the U.S. Army Air Force without notifying the Yankees. During his first seven years with the team, DiMaggio had smashed 219 home runs.

DiMaggio's salary went from an estimated $43,750 per year to $600 per year.

DiMaggio spent three seasons (1943–1945) in the prime of his career in the Army, mostly at the air base at Santa Ana, California. DiMaggio also served in Hawaii. He was released on September 14, 1945, as a sergeant.

February 26, 1935

Babe Ruth Is Released by the New York Yankees

After 15 years and 659 home runs with the New York Yankees, the team released George Herman "Babe" Ruth.[7] But the same day, he signed as a free agent with the Boston Bees (Braves).

---

7. Ruth is said to have wondered why he wasn't named manager of the Yankees. He was told, "If you can't manage *yourself*, how can you manage a team?"

MARCH

DID YOU KNOW?

The first player to hit at least one home run in four consecutive World Series was Mickey Mantle of the New York Yankees: 1955 (1), 1956 (3),[8] 1957 (1), and 1958 (2). Mantle played in 65 World Series games in 12 World Series. He homered in 16 of those games, smacking 18 round-trippers.

---

8. Mantle had a very good year in 1956. He won the American League Triple Crown and was the Most Valuable Player in the American League.

March 1, 1969

Mickey Mantle Retires

After 18 years (1951–1968) and 536 home runs, all for the Yankees, Mickey Mantle announced his retirement, saying, "I can't hit when I need to."

March 4, 1913

New York Yankees Train in Bermuda

The New York Yankees did something that no major-league team had ever done before: they held spring training outside the United States. The team prepared for the 1913 season in Bermuda. They hit 8 homers that year in the Deadball Era.

March 26, 1951

Mickey Mantle Hits a Ball More Than 500 Feet in an Exhibition Game

In the top of the first inning, 19-year old Mickey Mantle—just two years out of high school—batting lefty in an exhibition game against the University of Southern California team *before his major league career began*, hit a pitch from 6'5" "Tall" Tom Lovrich over the right-center-field wall. With three thousand people in attendance, the ball went onto the sideline of the adjacent football practice field. The spot where the ball bounced measured more than 500 feet from home plate.

Final score: Yankees 15, USC 1.

March 30, 2004

Jason Giambi Hits the First Yankees Home Run in Japan

At the Tokyo Dome (home of the Yomiuri Giants of the Japanese Central League) in front of 55 thousand people, the New York Yankees played the Tampa Bay Devil Rays in the teams' first regular-season major-league game in Japan. Prime Minister Junichiro Koizumi threw out the ceremonial first pitch to Hideki Matsui ("Godzilla"), who had been a superstar during his 10 years playing in Japan before becoming a Yankee.

In the top of the first inning, with Matsui on second base, Yankees first baseman Jason Giambi blasted a Victor Zambrano fastball over the left-field wall—the first Yankees home run in Japan.

Final Score: Tampa Bay 8, New York 3.

After the game, Rays shortstop Julio Lugo, who had doubled and scored, was voted the game's most valuable player and was awarded a million yen, about $10,000.

APRIL

DID YOU KNOW?

Roger Maris of the 1961 New York Yankees was the first player to hit at least 50 home runs in a season (61) but *not* hit .300. His batting average that year was .269.

April 2, 2003

Todd Zeile Homers for His 10th Team

Scene: SkyDome, Toronto, Canada

Attendance: 16,222

In the top of the first inning of the third game of the season, New York Yankees third baseman Todd Zeile[9] homered off Mark Hendrickson of the Toronto Blue Jays. So?

The Yankees were the 10th team for which Zeile hit a home run—a record. The others: the Rockies, Mets, Marlins, Rangers, Dodgers, Orioles, Cubs, Phillies, and Cardinals.

Final score: Yankees 9, Blue Jays 7.

Zeile added an 11th team, the Montreal Expos, in 2003.

April 6, 1974

Graig Nettles Hits a Home Run in the New York Yankees' Temporary Home, Shea Stadium

Scene: Shea Stadium, New York City

Attendance: 20,744

Yankee Stadium was built in 1923. By 1974, it was badly in need of renovations. So for the two years during which the renovations took, the Yankees played their home games at Shea Stadium, home of the New York Mets.

On Opening Day, Yankees third baseman Graig Nettles homered in the bottom of the fourth inning off Cleveland Indians pitcher Gaylord Perry, with Ron Blomberg on base.

Final score: Yankees 6, Indians 1.

---

9.   Zeile is one of the few major leaguers who was married to an Olympic gold-medal winner. She's Julianne McNamara, who won a gold medal on the uneven bars (tied with Ma Yanhong of China) at the 1984 Olympics in Los Angeles.

April 8, 2003

Hideki Matsui Hits a Grand Slam in His First Game at Yankee Stadium

Scene: Yankee Stadium, New York City
Attendance: 33,109 in subfreezing weather.

The Yankees had just paid twenty-eight-year-old free agent Hideki Matsui $21 million for three years to pry him away from the Yomiuri Giants, for whom he had smacked 50 home runs in 2002.

The press box and camera well were overflowing with reporters and photographers from American and Japanese media outlets. Matsui had been the biggest star in Japan.

Leading off the bottom of the second inning of the Yankees 2003 home opener against the Minnesota Twins, Matsui, playing left field, grounded out to second.

In the bottom of the fifth inning, Matsui faced Joe Mays. The Yankees had the bases loaded with Nick Johnson, Jason Giambi, and Bernie Williams.

As the fans chanted his name, Matsui crushed a 3–2 change-up, sending it 400 feet into the stands for a grand slam. With his father Masao in the stands, the Yankee Stadium crowd gave Matsui a 30-second standing ovation.

Final score: Yankees 7, Twins 3.

April 9, 1965

In an Exhibition Game, Mickey Mantle Hits the First Home Run in Texas—And the First Home Run Indoors

Scene: The Astrodome, Houston
Attendance: 47,876

Though it was just an exhibition game at the new home of the Houston Astros, the Houston Astrodome[10] was packed for its first game. President and Mrs. Lyndon Johnson were at the game, though they arrived late. In the top of the sixth inning, New York Yankees slugger Mickey Mantle, who batted in the leadoff spot and had the first hit in the Astrodome—a single in the first inning—smacked a Turk Farrell pitch over 400 feet into the center-field stands.

Final score: Astros 2, Yankees 1 in 12 innings.

April 10, 1976

We're *Not* in the Money

Scene: County Stadium, Milwaukee
Attendance: 10,871

There were no outs as the Milwaukee Brewers batted in the bottom of the ninth inning with the bases loaded with Robin Yount, Pedro Garcia, and Bobby Darwin. The Yankees led 9–6. Dave Pagan was on the mound for New York, with Don Money at the plate. The crowd was screaming.

New York first baseman Chris Chambliss called time and first-base umpire Jim McKean granted it, but Pagan apparently didn't hear him. When he delivered, Money blasted what looked like a walk-off grand slam into the left field seats.

But the homer was nullified by the timeout call, and the runners returned to their bases. When Pagan pitched again, Money hit a fly ball to right field.

Final score: Yankees 9, Brewers 7. The Brewers' subsequent protest was denied.

---

10. Touted as the "Eighth Wonder of the World."

April 13, 1939

Lou Gehrig's Final Home Runs

New York Yankees first baseman Lou Gehrig—"The Iron Horse"—homered in the second and ninth innings against the Brooklyn Dodgers in a spring-training game in Norfolk, Virginia. Those were the final home runs of Gehrig's 17-year (1923–1939) career, all with the New York Yankees, for whom Gehrig hit 493 homers.

Final score: Dodgers 14, Yankees 12.

April 13, 1978

Reg-Gie! Reg-Gie! Reg-Gie!

Scene: Yankee Stadium, New York City
Attendance: 44,667

In the bottom of the first inning of the New York Yankees' 1978 home opener, Reggie Jackson hit a three-run shot off Chicago White Sox pitcher Wilbur Wood. The ball was just out of the grasp of center fielder Chet Lemon at the 400-foot sign. This was Jackson's first swing of the bat since he hit 3 home runs in Game Six of the 1977 World Series in New York on October 18.

Reggie Jackson

The game was delayed five minutes while the grounds crew picked up the hundreds of Reggie! candy bars—72,000 of which had been given away—that were thrown on the field by ecstatic fans.

Final score: Yankees 4, White Sox 2.

April 15, 1976

Dan Ford Hits the First Home Run in the Renovated Yankee Stadium

Scene: Yankee Stadium, New York City
Attendance: 52,613

On April 15, 1976, the Yankees played their home opener against the Minnesota Twins at the newly renovated Yankee Stadium. In the top of the first inning, with Jerry Terrell on base, "Disco" Dan Ford connected off Yankees pitcher Rudy May—the first home run at the newly refurbished stadium.

Final score: Yankees 11, Twins 4.

The first Yankees home run at the renovated stadium was hit by catcher Thurman Munson the next day, April 16, in the bottom of the first inning off Twins hurler Jim Hughes.

April 16, 1946

Joe DiMaggio Hits His First Home Run in More Than 3½ Years

Scene: Shibe Park, Philadelphia
Attendance: 37,472

After three years in the U.S. Army Air Force during World War II, New York Yankees center fielder Joe DiMaggio was back. On Opening Day of the first post war season, DiMaggio came to bat in the sixth inning with Tommy Henrich on base.

The pitcher was Russ Christopher of the Philadelphia Athletics.

DiMaggio smashed his first home run since September 27, 1942. He hit 25 in 1946.

Final score: Yankees 5, Athletics 0. The Yankees played the entire game with just their starting lineup.

Joe DiMaggio

April 16, 2009

Jorge Posada Hits the First Yankees Home Run at the New Yankee Stadium II

Scene:　　　　Yankee Stadium II, New York City
Attendance:　48,271 (Capacity 51,800)

Yankees legend Yogi Berra threw out the ceremonial first pitch for the New York Yankees home opener at their brand new ballpark, Yankee Stadium II, across the street from the original Yankee Stadium. The bat that Babe Ruth used to hit the first home run at the original Yankee Stadium, borrowed for the occasion from its owner, was placed on home plate before Derek Jeter led off the bottom of the first inning.

The first home run at the new park was hit by Yankees catcher Jorge Posada. He batted with two outs in the fifth inning, facing Cliff Lee of the Cleveland Indians. Posada sent the pitch into the center-field stands near Monument Park.

In the seventh inning, facing Dámaso Marté, Cleveland's Grady Sizemore hit the first grand slam in the new stadium. Ben Francisco, Kelly Shoppach, and Trevor Crowe were on base. A Yankees fan threw it back onto the field.

Final Score: Indians 10, Yankees 2.

April 17, 1953

Mickey Mantle Hits a Monster Home Run

Scene: Griffith Stadium, Washington, D.C.

Attendance: 4,206

In the fourth game of the 1953 season, 21-year-old New York Yankees center fielder Mickey Mantle hit his first home run of the season—one for the ages. He batted righty in the top of the fifth inning, with two outs facing Washington Senators pitcher Chuck Stobbs. With Yogi Berra on base, Mantle grabbed a random bat[11] and hit a pitch over the 55-foot wall in left field for a 2-run homer. The ball went out of the stadium and landed in a backyard at 434 Oakdale Street—565 feet away—a true tape-measure home run.

In the ninth inning, Mantle had one of the longest bunts in history. The ball landed in front of second base. Mantle, one of the fastest baserunners in the history of the majors, landed on first.

Final score: Yankees 7, Senators 3.

April 18, 1923

Babe Ruth Hits the First Home Run Ever at Yankee Stadium

Scene: Yankee Stadium, New York City

Attendance: 74,200[12]

---

11. The one he picked was a Loren Babe model. During his two-year major-league career, Babe, a native of Pisgah, Iowa, hit two home runs. It's not the bat.

12. An estimated 25 thousand fans were turned away. This broke the previous attendance record of 47,373 set in Game Two of the 1916 World Series at Boston's Braves Field by 26,827.

The Opening Day festivities in the very first game at Yankee Stadium,[13] the Yankees' new home, started with the raising of the 1922 American League championship pennant. The Seventh Regiment Band, led by John Phillip Sousa, played the National Anthem.

With Yankees Whitey Witt on third and "Jumping" Joe Dugan on first with two outs, Babe Ruth came to bat in the bottom of the third inning.

Babe Ruth

On a 2–2 pitch from Boston Red Sox pitcher Howard Ehmke, Ruth homered into the right-field bleachers, the first of the league-leading 41 home runs he'd hit that season.

Six thousand five hundred eighty-one regular-season games were played at Yankee Stadium during its 85-year history, 1923 to 2008. Construction cost Jacob Ruppert, the team's owner, $2.4 million. By contrast, Yankee Stadium II, which opened on April 16, 2009, cost approximately $1.3 billion.

Final score: Yankees 4, Red Sox 1.

April 19, 1948

Allie Reynolds Hits . . . A Home Run

Scene: Griffith Stadium, Washington, D.C.
Attendance: 31,728

In an Opening Day game in which President Harry S. Truman threw out the ceremonial first pitch, thirty-one-year-old Yankees pitcher Allie Reynolds—also known as

---

13. The dimensions of Yankee Stadium were said to have been tailored for the left-handed power swing of Babe Ruth. Hence Yankee Stadium was known as "The House that Ruth Built."

"The Super Chief,[14]" a name given to him by Yankees broadcaster Mel Allen—hit the only home run of his 13-year (1942–1954) career, a blast that went over the fence in left field. The three-run clout came in the top of the first inning off Washington Senators pitcher Early Wynn.

But Reynolds was running, not watching the ball, so he didn't see the ball clear the fence. Reynolds stopped at second base, believing that the Washington Senators were trying to trick him into getting off base. Eventually, he completed his trot around the bases.

Final score: Yankees 12, Senators 4.

April 20, 1988

Claudell Washington Hits the Yankees' 10,000th Home Run

Scene: Hubert H. Humphrey Metrodome, Minneapolis
Attendance: 22,369

In the top of the ninth inning, thirty-three-year old Claudell Washington[15] of the New York Yankees, using a Rick Cerone autograph model bat,[16] pinch-hit a home run 448 feet to the upper deck in right field off Minnesota Twins pitcher Jeff

---

14. If Reynolds's nickname is derived from the name of the Santa Fe Railroad's flagship train "The Super Chief," a symbol of power, traveling daily from Chicago to Los Angeles, it's great. If it refers to Reynolds's Native American—heritage-he was part Creek Indian—it is not politically correct. Most ballplayers of American Indian heritage were nicknamed "Chief." See, e.g., John "Chief" Meyers, Moses "Chief" Yellowhorse, and Charles "Chief" Zimmer.

15. Washington is one of 34 future major leaguers who attended California's Berkeley High School.

16. Washington's own bats had not yet arrived.

Reardon—the 10,000th home run in Yankee history. The Yankees were the first team to record 10,000 round-trippers. Final score: Yankees 7, Twins 6.

April 22, 1915

Luke Boone Hits the First Home Run Wearing Pinstripes

Scene: The Polo Grounds, New York City
Attendance: 7,000

In 1915, the New York Yankees adopted a new uniform for home games: pinstripes. In the bottom of the seventh inning of the 1915 home opener, Yankees second baseman Luke (given name: Lute[17]) Boone became the first Yankee to homer in pinstripes. The pitcher was Jim Shaw of the Washington Senators. Final score: Senators 5, Yankees 1.

April 22, 2007

The Boston Red Sox Hit Four Consecutive Home Runs

Scene: Fenway Park, Boston
Attendance: 36,905

Sebern "Chase" Wright of the New York Yankees was on the mound in the bottom of the third inning when Manny Ramirez, J. D. Drew, Mike Lowell, and Jason Varitek of the Boston Red Sox hit consecutive home runs.

---

17. Undoubtedly a friend of Frank Viola, Steve Sax, Sam Horn, Buddy Bell, Anthony Bass, Fiddler Corridon, Jimmy Key, and Toots Schultz.

For Drew, this was nothing new—he'd been one of four Dodgers to hit consecutive home runs on September 18, 2006. Final score: Boston 7, New York 6.

April 23, 2000

Bernie Williams and Jorge Posada Switch-Hit Home Runs in the Same Game

Scene: SkyDome, Toronto
Attendance: 20,485

In the top of the first inning, with two outs and Derek Jeter on base, New York Yankees center fielder Bernie Williams, batting lefty, homered off Toronto Blue Jays pitcher Frank Castillo.

In the second inning, Yankees catcher Jorge Posada, batting lefty, cranked a solo shot, also off Castillo.

By the fourth inning, the new Blue Jays pitcher was Clayton Andrews, a lefty. With Jeter and Paul O'Neill aboard, Williams batted righty and homered. After Tino Martinez singled, Posada—also batting righty—homered.

Williams and Posada were the first teammates each to switch-hit home runs in the same game.

Final score: Yankees 10, Blue Jays 7.

April 25, 1942

Jimmie Foxx Hits His Last Home Run Against the Yankees

Scene: Fenway Park, Boston
Attendance: 19,538

Lefty Gomez was on the mound for the New York Yankees when Boston Red Sox slugger Jimmie Foxx led off the bottom of the 5th inning with a round-tripper. This was Foxx's 14th career home run off Gomez, and his 70th and final home run against Yankees pitching. Seventy-five years after this clout, nobody has hit more homers against the Yankees.

Eleven future Hall of Famers were on the field for this game: Foxx, Gomez, Joe DiMaggio, Phil Rizzuto, Ted Williams, Bobby Doerr, Joe Gordon, Bill Dickey, Charles "Red" Ruffing, and managers Joe McCarthy of the Yankees and Joe Cronin of the Red Sox.

DiMaggio's brother Dom was the center fielder for the Red Sox.

Final Score: Red Sox 4, Yankees 2.

April 26, 1931

Lou Gehrig Loses a Home Run

Scene: Griffith Stadium, Washington, D.C.
Attendance: 14,000

With two outs and Lyn Lary on base in the top of the first inning, first baseman Lou Gehrig of the New York Yankees homered off Frederick "Firpo" Marberry of the Washington Senators. The ball cleared the fence in center field but bounced back onto the field where it was caught by Harry Rice in center field. Lary thought the ball was caught for the final out of the inning and ran to the dugout instead of scoring from third base. Gehrig was called out by umpire Bill McGowan for passing a runner on the basepaths.

Gehrig tied Babe Ruth for the 1931 home run crown with 46 and had to settle for "only" 185 RBIs, still the second best ever.[18]

Ten future Hall of Famers appeared in this game: umpires McGowan and Tommy Connolly, Gehrig, Earle Combs, Red Ruffing, Tony Lazzeri, Joe Sewell, Sam Rice, Heinie Manush, and Joe Cronin.

Final score: Senators 9, Yankees 7.

April 28, 1956

Mickey Mantle Misses a Home Run

Scene: Fenway Park, Boston
Attendance: 27,357

With Jerry Coleman on second base in the top of the eighth inning, New York Yankees slugger Mickey Mantle, in his Triple Crown season, lifted a towering blast to the bleachers in Fenway Park's center field. A number of fans chased it, but it bounced back on the field. Umpire Eddie Rommel ruled— incorrectly—that the ball did *not* land in the stands, but hit the top of the wall. When Yankees manager Casey Stengel argued, he was ejected. Mantle had to settle for a triple.

Final score: Red Sox 6, Yankees 4.

April 28, 1963

A Home Run for Whitey Ford

Scene: Yankee Stadium, New York City
Attendance: 22,346

---

18. Hack Wilson's record of 191 RBIs, set in 1930, may last forever.

During his 16-year Hall of Fame career (1950, 1953–1967) as a pitcher for the New York Yankees, New York City native Edward "Whitey" Ford—"The Chairman of the Board"— won 236 games while losing only 106. He led the American League in wins three times; led in ERA, starts, innings pitched, and shutouts twice; was an eight-time All-Star; and won the Cy Young Award in 1961.

On this date, he did something very rare: Ford hit the third and final home run of his career.

In the bottom of the fourth inning, Ford faced Jim "Mudcat" Grant[19] of the Cleveland Indians. Ford hit a home run— the first home run by a Yankees pitcher since 1960.

Final score: Yankees 5, Indians 0. Ford got the win.

April 28, 2017

Jacoby Ellsbury Hits the 100th Home Run of His Career—And It's His First Grand Slam

Scene: Yankee Stadium, New York City
Attendance: 36,912

Through 2017, only 869 players have hit at least 100 career home runs. The first man whose 100th career home run was also his first grand slam was Bryce Harper of the Washington Nationals. He hit it on April 14, 2016.

The 2017 season was Jacoby Ellsbury's 11th in the major leagues, and his fourth with the New York Yankees.[20]

---

19. Grant is the only major leaguer from Lacoochie, Florida.
20. Ellsbury, the first major leaguer who is part Navajo, is the only native of Madras, Oregon, to play in the major leagues.

On April 28, 2017, Ellsbury became the second player in major-league history whose 100th career home run was his first career grand slam. Austin Romine, Chase Headley, and Matt Holliday were on base in the bottom of the seventh inning, when Ellsbury, playing center field, faced Baltimore Orioles pitcher Vidal Nuño. Ellsbury's round-tripper ended up in the right-field seats.

Final score: Yankees 14, Orioles 11 in 10 innings. There were 8 home runs in the game, which Baltimore once led by 8.

MAY

May 5, 1913

Jeff Sweeney Hits the First New York Yankees Home Run

Scene: The Polo Grounds, New York City

The 1913 New York Yankees (previously known as the Highlanders) were not a slugging team. They hit only 8 home runs all season. Jeff Sweeney accounted for 2 of them.

The first home run hit by a player who was known as a "Yankee" was a solo shot by Sweeney off Philadelphia Athletics pitcher Eddie Plank, a future Hall of Famer, in the bottom of the fifth inning.

Final score: A's 8, Yankees 1.

May 5, 1922

Construction Begins on Yankee Stadium

The new home of the Yankees took less than a year to build. The first game was played there on April 18, 1923. At the Polo Grounds in 1922, the Yankees hit 95 home runs. In 1923, in their new home, the team hit 105.

May 7, 1955

Elston Howard Hits His First Home Run for the New York Yankees

Scene: Fenway Park, Boston
Attendance: 29,925

Jackie Robinson broke the color line in Major League Baseball in 1947. But the New York Yankees did not sign a black player until 1955—Elston Howard. Howard hit his first home run in the top of the seventh inning off Boston Red Sox pitcher Tom Hurd.

Final score: Yankees 9, Red Sox 6.

During his 13 years (1955–1967) with the Yankees, Howard clouted 161 round-trippers.

May 12, 1925

Lawrence Peter "Yogi" Berra Is Born

Yogi Berra, who hit 358 home runs for the Yankees from 1946–1963, and later managed the team, was born in St. Louis, Missouri. In a record 14 World Series, Berra hit 12 home runs. A standout catcher, Berra was voted the Most Valuable Player in the American League in 1951, 1954, and 1955. Berra managed the Yankees in 1964 (when the Yankees won the American League pennant), and 1984–85.

Yogi Berra

May 12, 1978

Amos Otis Hits a Walk-Off Inside-the-Park Home Run

Scene: Royals Stadium, Kansas City
Attendance: 33,061

The Yankees led the Kansas City Royals 3–2 in the bottom of the ninth inning when Rich "Goose" Gossage came in to pitch for New York. Darrell Porter was on base. The batter was Amos Otis.

After Otis hit a routine fly ball, Yankees center fielder Mickey "Mick the Quick" Rivers and right fielder Reggie Jackson collided in center field, causing the ball to drop. Meanwhile, Otis circled the bases for a walk-off inside-the-park home run.

Final score: Kansas City 4, New York 3.

May 13, 1955

Mickey Mantle Switch-Hits Home Runs for the First Time

Scene: Yankee Stadium, New York City
Attendance: 7,177

The handful of fans who showed up at Yankee Stadium were in for a real treat. Twenty-three-year-old New York Yankees center fielder Mickey Mantle, batting lefty and using an Enos

Mickey Mantle

Slaughter bat, homered in both the first and fifth innings off Detroit Tigers pitcher Steve Gromek.

In the eighth inning, Mantle turned around to bat righty to face Bob Miller. Using a Bill Skowron bat this time, Mantle homered again—the first of 10 times Mantle switch-hit home runs in the same game.

Final score: Yankees 5, Tigers 2.

May 14, 1967

Mickey Mantle Hits Career Home Run Number 500

Scene: Yankee Stadium, New York City
Attendance: 18,872

With two outs in the bottom of the seventh inning, thirty-five-year-old New York Yankee Mickey Mantle, playing first base, came to bat against Baltimore Orioles pitcher Stu Miller[21] for the first time. On a 3–2 pitch, Mantle smashed a home run into the right field stands for his fourth homer of the season—the 500th blast of his career.[22]

In the top of the eighth, Mantle—still overcome with emotion after his historic home run—made an error that cost the Yankees a run. Mantle's home run proved to be the difference in the game.

Final score: Yankees 6, Orioles 5.

---

21. Stu Miller was memorably blown off the pitcher's mound and called for a balk during the ninth inning of the first 1961 All-Star Game on July 1 at San Francisco's Candlestick Park.

22. The ball was caught by eighteen-year-old Yankees fan Louis DeFillipo—a center fielder who switched to first base after Mantle did. DeFillipo presented the ball to Mantle outside the Yankees' clubhouse. In exchange, Mantle gave him a season pass to Yankee Stadium and other items.

May 16, 1953

Pitcher Tommy Byrne Pinch-Hits a Grand Slam

Scene: Yankee Stadium, New York City
Attendance: 22,966

In the top of the ninth inning of a game against the New York Yankees, Chicago White Sox pitcher and former Yankee Tommy Byrne—a lefty—pinch-hit for Vern Stephens. The bases were loaded with Saturnino "Minnie" Minoso, Tom Wright, and "Jungle" Jim Rivera. The pitcher was Ewell "The Whip" Blackwell.

The decision to pinch-hit worked, as Byrne smacked a grand slam into the lower right-field seats.

Final score: White Sox 5, Yankees 3.

May 17, 2002

Jason Giambi Hits a Walk-Off Grand Slam in the 14th Inning

Scene: Yankee Stadium, New York City
Attendance: 39,470

The Minnesota Twins were ahead 12–9 going into the bottom of the 14th inning in a game that took 5 hours and 45 minutes. Shane Spencer, Derek Jeter, and Bernie Williams were on base when Yankees designated hitter Jason Giambi stepped up to face Mike Trombley, the eighth Twins pitcher of the game.

Before this game, only one Yankee had hit a walk-off grand slam with the Yankees behind by exactly 3 runs: on

September 24, 1925—*77 years previously*—when the Chicago White Sox led 5–2 in the bottom of the 10th inning. Facing George "Sarge" Connally with Wally Pipp, Earle Combs, and Mark Koenig aboard, Babe Ruth clouted a grand slam before a crowd of only 1,000.

On that day in 2002, Giambi joined him, hitting his ninth home run of the season—a walk-off grand slam.

Final score: Yankees 13, Twins 12.

May 18, 1946

Reggie Jackson Is Born

Reggie Jackson, who hit 563 home runs during his 20-year (1967–1987) career with the Kansas City (1967) and Oakland Athletics (1968–1975, 1987), Baltimore Orioles (1976), New York Yankees (1977–1981), and California Angels (1982–1986), was born in Abington, Pennsylvania.

May 22, 1930

Lou Gehrig Becomes the First Player to Hit Three Home Runs in a Game Three Times

Scene: Shibe Park, Philadelphia
Attendance: 24,000

In the second game of a doubleheader against the Philadelphia Athletics, New York Yankees first baseman Lou Gehrig hit three home runs in one game (off Bill Shores, Eddie Rommel, and Glenn Liebhardt) for the third time—the first player to do so. The first two times were June 23, 1927, and May 4, 1929.

Final score: Yankees 11, White Sox 9.

Lou Gehrig

May 22, 2009

Raúl Ibañez Hits a Ball 477 Feet

Scene: Yankee Stadium II, New York City
Attendance: 46,288

Jimmy Rollins of the Philadelphia Phillies homered on the first pitch of the game, from A. J. Burnett of the New York Yankees.

In the top of the seventh inning, Phillies third baseman Raúl Ibañez, a native New Yorker, blasted a pitch from Yankees pitcher Chien-Ming Wang 477 feet to right field.

Other home runs in this game were hit by Phillies Carlos Ruiz and Jayson Werth, and Yankees Alex Rodriguez, Derek Jeter, and Mark Teixeira.

Final score: Phillies 7, Yankees 3.

May 23, 1948

Joe DiMaggio Blasts 3 Home Runs

Scene: Cleveland Stadium

Attendance: 78,431

During Game One of a doubleheader, with Tommy Henrich on base in the fourth inning, Joltin' Joe DiMaggio smashed a home run off Cleveland Indians pitching ace Bob Feller.

In the sixth inning, DiMaggio smacked a three-run blast with Henrich and Charlie "King Kong" Keller on base, also off Feller.

In the eighth inning, DiMaggio hit a solo homer off reliever Bob Muncrief.

The Yankees had been down 0–4, but came back to win 6–5.

Joe DiMaggio

May 24, 1932

Babe Ruth Homers off Rube Walberg

Scene: Yankee Stadium, New York City

Babe Ruth's first home run off George "Rube" Walberg[23] was a three-run blast on July 24, 1923. Ruth was a Yankee, and Walberg was with the Philadelphia Athletics.

Nine years later, on May 24, 1932, in the bottom of the first inning, Ruth smashed a solo homer off Walberg, still with the A's.

This was the 17th and final home run Ruth hit off Walberg—the most off any pitcher.

The Yankees' starting nine played the entire game.

Seven future Hall of Famers appeared in this game: Ruth, Lou Gehrig, Lefty Gomez, Bill Dickey, Joe Sewell, Al Simmons, and Jimmie Foxx.

Final score: Yankees 3, Athletics 1.

May 24, 1936

Tony Lazzeri Hits Two Grand Slams in One Game

Scene: Shibe Park, Philadelphia
Attendance: 8,000

The New York Yankees were in first place[24] on May 24, 1936, when they faced the seventh-place Philadelphia Athletics. Thirty-two-year-old Yankees second baseman Tony "Poosh

---

23. Walberg is a native of Pine City, Minnesota.
24. The Yankees won the World Series in 1936, 1937, 1938, and 1939. Joe DiMaggio, a twenty-one-year old rookie in 1936, became the only player ever to win world championships in his first four years in the majors.

'Em Up" Lazzeri came to bat in the second inning against A's pitcher George Turbeville. Bill Dickey, Ben Chapman, and George "Twinkle-toes" Selkirk were on base. Lazzeri homered—the 7th grand slam of his career.

Tony Lazzeri

In the fifth inning, Lazzeri batted again with the bases loaded (Dickey, Chapman, and Selkirk). This time, the pitcher was Herman Fink. Lazzeri homered again. Lazzeri became the first player to hit 2 grand slams in one game.

Batting eighth, Lazzeri had 2 grand slams, another home run in the seventh inning, and barely missed a 4th homer in the eighth inning. He had to settle for a triple and 11 RBIs—an American League record that stood until 2014.

Lazzeri's 3 homers matched the 3 he had hit in a doubleheader the previous day—giving him an American League-record 6 homers in two days.

Those were Lazzeri's only grand slams of the season.

Lazzeri's 3 home runs and 11 RBIs overshadowed the home runs teammate Frank Crosetti hit in the seventh and eighth innings.

Final score: Yankees 25, A's 2.

May 25, 1937

Mickey Cochrane's Final Home Run

Scene: Yankee Stadium, New York City
Attendance: 15,026

Thirty-four-year-old Mickey Cochrane, one of the greatest catchers of all time, was the player-manager of the Detroit Tigers. During his thirteen-year (1925–1937) career, he hit 119 home runs, including a personal best of 23 in 1932.

With two outs in the top of the third inning, he homered off New York Yankees pitcher Irving "Bump" Hadley.

Hadley was still on the mound when Cochrane came up to bat again in the fifth inning. A pitch hit Cochrane in the temple, fracturing his skull in three places[25]. Cochrane lay in a coma for 10 days. He recovered but never played again.

Hall of Famers on the field for this game included Cochrane, Hank Greenberg, Goose Goslin, Joe DiMaggio, Lou Gehrig, Bill Dickey, Tony Lazzeri, and Yankees manager Joe McCarthy.

Final score: Yankees 4, Tigers 3.

May 28, 1934

A Record 16 Back-to-Back Home Runs for Babe Ruth and Lou Gehrig

The pair of players who hit the most back-to-back home runs in baseball history are Babe Ruth and Lou Gehrig. The two were teammates on the New York Yankees from 1923 to 1934. During that time, they hit back-to-back home runs a record 16 times.

The last time Ruth and Gehrig hit back-to-back home runs was in the seventh inning on May 28, 1934 (both off Jack Knott), in a 13–9 Yankees victory over the St. Louis Browns. New York collected 21 hits, including homers by Ruth, Gehrig (2), Tony Lazzeri, and Otto "Jack" Saltzgaver.[26]

Ruth and Gehrig's record remains unbroken.

---

25. This was years before the advent of batting helmets.
26. Saltzgaver is the only major leaguer who was born in Croton, Iowa.

May 30, 1938

The Yankees Take on the Red Sox in a Doubleheader at Yankee Stadium

Scene: Yankee Stadium, New York City
Attendance: 81,891

As every kid who has ever jumped into a swimming pool knows, it's no good unless somebody is *watching*. A record Yankee Stadium Memorial Day crowd of *81,891* fans were watching this day as the Yankees hosted the Boston Red Sox for a doubleheader. An additional 6,000 fans were turned away.

No home runs were hit in the first game.

In Game Two, Yankees first baseman Lou Gehrig homered in the bottom of the sixth inning with Joe DiMaggio on base. The pitcher was Jack Wilson.

Ten future Hall of Famers were on the field: umpires Cal Hubbard and Bill McGowan, plus Gehrig, DiMaggio, Bill Dickey, Lefty Gomez, Jimmie Foxx, and Bobby Doerr. The Red Sox manager was Joe Cronin. Joe McCarthy managed the Yankees.

Final score: Yankees 5, Red Sox 4.

May 31, 1944

Al Unser Hits a Pinch-Hit Walk-Off Grand Slam

Scene: Briggs Stadium, Detroit
Attendance: 2,941—49,475 seats remained empty

It is unknown how many of the "crowd" of 2,941 fans stayed until the final play of the game. Those who did had a thrill.

With two outs and the bases loaded (Pinky Higgins, Jimmy Outlaw, and Johnny Gorsica) in the bottom of the ninth inning, Al Unser[27] of the Detroit Tigers connected for his only home run of the season—a pinch-hit walk-off grand slam.

Final score: Tigers 6, Yankees 2.

---

27. Unser is the only native of Morrisonville, Illinois, to play major-league baseball.

JUNE

June 3, 1932

Six Future Hall of Famers Homer in One Game, Including Gehrig with 4

Scene: Shibe Park, Philadelphia
Attendance: 5,000

A record six future Hall of Famers hit home runs in this game. Also, Yankees first baseman Lou Gehrig became the first player to hit 4 home runs in a single game.[28]

Gehrig, age twenty-eight, hit the first home run of the game in the top of the first inning off George Earnshaw[29] of the Philadelphia Athletics with Jack Saltzgaver on base.

In the bottom of the inning, the A's Mickey Cochrane homered off Johnny Allen with Max Bishop on base.

Gehrig hit his second home run, a solo shot, in the fourth inning, again off Earnshaw.

Yankees Earle Combs, Babe Ruth, and Gehrig homered in the top of the fifth, all off Earnshaw.

In the top of the seventh inning, Gehrig hit his record-breaking 4th homer of the game off Roy Mahaffey.

Yankees second baseman Tony Lazzeri hit a grand slam in the ninth inning off Eddie Rommel, scoring Myril Hoag, Ben Chapman, and Bill Dickey.

Jimmie Foxx homered for the A's in the bottom of the ninth inning off Vernon "Lefty" Gomez in a game that saw 33 runs and 36 hits—including 9 home runs.

Final score: Yankees 20, A's 13.

---

28. Gehrig also had an error in the fourth inning, dropping a fly ball.
29. Gehrig and Earnshaw are both New York City natives.

June 3, 2000

Chris Turner Homers at Turner Field

Scene: Turner Field, Atlanta
Attendance: 48,423

New York Yankees catcher Chris *Turner* led off the top of the third inning with a home run off Greg Maddux of the Atlanta Braves at *Turner* Field.[30]

Final score: Braves 11, Yankees 7.

June 3, 2017

Four New York Yankees Homer in One Inning

Scene: Rogers Centre, Toronto
Attendance: 47,226

New York Yankees center fielder Brett Gardner led off the top of the eighth inning with a home run to right field off Jason Grilli of the Toronto Blue Jays. After Aaron Hicks and Aaron Judge were retired, Matt Holliday blasted a ball to center field, Starlin Castro hit one to left center, and Didi Gregorius clouted a 3–2 slider to right, all off Grilli. That marked 3 consecutive home runs, and 4 in one inning.

Final score: New York 7, Toronto 0.

---

30. Boston's Yank Terry never homered at Yankee Stadium. Charlie Comiskey never homered at Comiskey Park. Daryl Boston did not homer for the Boston Braves or the Boston Red Sox. Houston Jiménez never homered in Houston. Steve Phoenix didn't hit any home runs in Phoenix. Shea Hillenbrand never homered at Shea Stadium. But Claudell Washington *did* homer in Seattle, Washington.

June 6, 1944

No Home Runs Are Hit

No home runs were hit in Major League Baseball because no games were played. It's D-Day, the day the Allies invaded Normandy.

June 8, 2005

Alex Rodriguez—The Youngest Player to Hit 400 Home Runs

Scene: Miller Park, Milwaukee
Attendance: 37,586

In the top of the first inning, New York Yankees third baseman Alex Rodriguez homered off Milwaukee Brewers pitcher Chris Capuano with two outs and Gary Sheffield on base.

In the eighth inning, Rodriguez went deep off Jorge de la Rosa, the 400th home run of his career.

At age 29 years, 316 days, Rodriguez became the youngest player ever to hit 400 home runs.

Final score: Yankees 12, Brewers 3.

June 10, 2002

Marcus Thames Homers on the First Pitch of His Career

Scene: Yankee Stadium, New York City
Attendance: 45,698

In the bottom of the third inning, with Shane Spencer on second, twenty-five-year-old New York Yankees right fielder

Marcus Thames[31] made his major-league debut facing Arizona Diamondbacks pitcher Randy Johnson. Using Enrique Wilson's bat, on the first pitch he ever saw in the majors—a high fastball—Thames hit a home run to left-center field.

Final score: Yankees 7, Diamondbacks 5.

June 18, 2005

Derek Jeter Hits His Only Grand Slam

Scene: Yankee Stadium, New York City
Attendance: 55,284

Shortstop Derek Jeter hit 2 home runs in this game. The second was a solo shot in the eighth inning off Chicago Cubs pitcher Cliff Bartosh.[32]

But Jeter's *1st* home run of the day, before a packed house at Yankee Stadium, in the sixth inning with Jorge Posada, Bernie Williams, and Robinson Cano on base, went into the left-center-field stands—the only grand slam of Jeter's 20-year (1995–2014) career.[33] The pitcher was Joe Borowski.

Final score: Yankees 8, Cubs 1.

June 19, 1903

Lou Gehrig Is Born

Lou Gehrig—"The Iron Horse"—was born in New York City, weighing nearly 14 pounds! During his 17-year (1923–1939) career with the New York Yankees, Gehrig hit 493

---

31. Thames is the only major leaguer born in Louisville, Mississippi.
32. Bartosh is from West, Texas.
33. 260 career home runs, 1 grand slam.

home runs. That was the record for most home runs by a first baseman until Mark McGwire broke the record when he hit home run number 494 as a first baseman in 1999.

June 19, 1977

Carl Yastrzemski Blasts a Titanic Home Run

Scene: Fenway Park, Boston
Attendance: 34,750

In the bottom of the eighth inning, Jim Rice of the Boston Red Sox homered. The next batter was left fielder Carl Yastrzemski.

Yastrzemski hit a ball about 460 feet that struck the facing of the roof in right field by the bleachers—the only ball ever hit that far at Fenway Park. One batter later, George "Boomer" Scott also homered. All three came off New York Yankees pitcher Dick "Dirt" Tidrow.

Final score: Red Sox 11, Yankees 1.

June 19, 2015

Alex Rodriguez's 3,000th Hit Is a Home Run

Scene: Yankee Stadium II, New York City
Attendance: 44,588

In the bottom of the first inning, New York Yankees designated hitter Alex Rodriguez—a New York City native—blasted his 3,000th hit, a solo home run to the right-field stands off Detroit Tigers pitcher Justin Verlander.

Final score: Yankees 7, Tigers 2.

June 1–June 22, 1941

The New York Yankees Homer in 18 Consecutive Games

Scene: Yankee Stadium, New York City
Attendance: 27,072

Joe DiMaggio's sixth-inning home run off Detroit Tigers pitcher Hal Newhouser extended two important streaks. First, it came in the middle of DiMaggio's 56-game hitting streak.

It also marked the 18th straight game in which the Yankees had hit at least one home run—a record.

Eight future Hall of Famers appeared in this game: DiMaggio, Yankees manager Joe McCarthy, Newhouser, Charlie Gehringer, Phil Rizzuto, Red Ruffing, Joe Gordon, and Bill Dickey.

Final score: Yankees 5, Tigers 4.

June 23, 1950

Most Home Runs Ever in One Game

Scene: Briggs Stadium, Detroit
Attendance: 51,400

The New York Yankees hit 6 (Hank Bauer-2, Yogi Berra, Jerry Coleman, Joe DiMaggio, and Tommy Henrich) home runs in this game—usually enough to win.

But the Detroit Tigers hit 5 (Paul "Dizzy" Trout, Jerry Priddy, Vic Wertz, and Walter "Hoot" Evers-2), including a walk-off blast by Evers.

The combined total of 11 home runs in one game is a record.

Final score: Tigers 10, Yankees 9.

June 24, 1936

Joe DiMaggio Hits Two Home Runs in One Inning

Scene: Comiskey Park, Chicago
Attendance: 7,000

In 1936, twenty-one-year-old New York Yankees rookie out-fielder Joe DiMaggio hit .323 with 15 triples—the most in the majors—and connected for 29 home runs. That stood as the Yankees rookie record for 81 years, until broken by Aaron Judge on July 7, 2017, when he hit his 30th of the season (and ultimately hit 52 that season). The 1936 Yankees were loaded with future Hall of Famers: DiMaggio, Bill Dickey, Lou Gehrig, Tony Lazzeri, Red Ruffing, and Lefty Gomez. In 1938, DiMaggio became the first player to win a World Championship in each of his first three seasons in the major leagues.

Joe DiMaggio

In the fifth inning, DiMaggio did something that no Yankee had ever done before: he blasted 2 home runs in one inning.

In an inning in which the Yankees scored 10 runs, DiMaggio homered off Chicago White Sox pitcher Ray Phelps with Red Rolfe on base.

After the Yankees batted around, DiMaggio came to bat again, this time facing Chicago native Russell "Red" Evans with Frank Crosetti and Pat Malone on base. DiMaggio homered again.

The Yankees played the entire game with just their starting nine.

Final score: Yankees 18, White Sox 11.

June 24, 1962

Jack Reed Homers in the 22nd Inning

Scene: Tiger Stadium, Detroit
Attendance: 35,368

The New York Yankees were tied at 7 with the Detroit Tigers after six innings. Then they played another *15* scoreless innings in a game that featured 43 players—including eight pinch-hitters and 14 pitchers—in the longest Yankees game ever.

In the top of the 22nd inning, with Roger Maris on base and Phil Regan on the mound, right fielder Jack Reed[34] hit the only home run of his career to give the Yankees a 2-run lead. When the Tigers failed to score in the bottom of the inning, after *seven hours*, the game was over.

---

34. Reed is a native of Silver City, Mississippi.

Yankees catcher Yogi Berra was behind the plate for all 22 innings.

Final score: Yankees 9, Tigers 7.

June 28, 1939

The New York Yankees Hit 13 Home Runs in a Doubleheader

Scene: Shibe Park, Philadelphia
Attendance: 21,612

In the first game of a doubleheader against the Philadelphia Athletics, Bill Dickey, George Selkirk, Joe Gordon, and Tommy Henrich all homered for the Yankees. Joe DiMaggio and Ellsworth "Babe" Dahlgren hit two each, for a total of 8 Yankee homers.

Joe DiMaggio

Final score: Yankees 23, A's 2.

In Game Two, the Yankees added another 5 round-trippers—one by Frank Crosetti, two by Gordon, and 1 each from DiMaggio and Dahlgren.

The combined 13 home runs set the major-league record for most home runs by one team in a doubleheader—a record that still stands as of the end of the 2017 season.

Final score: Yankees 10, A's 0.

JUNE 28, 1949

A Home Run for Joe DiMaggio

Scene: Fenway Park, Boston
Attendance: 36,228

On November 11, 1948, New York Yankees slugger Joe DiMaggio underwent surgery at Johns Hopkins Hospital in Baltimore to remove painful bone spurs from his right heel.

On the morning of June 28, 1949, for the first time since his operation six-and-a-half months before, DiMaggio woke up with no pain in his right foot. Phil Rizzuto was on base with two outs in the top of the third inning, when DiMaggio batted for the second time in 1949. He smashed a home run off Boston Red Sox pitcher Mickey McDermott. DiMaggio's younger brother Dom was the Red Sox center fielder.

Final score: Yankees 5, Red Sox 4.

JULY

DID YOU KNOW?

Pitcher Dave Eiland broke in with the Yankees on August 3, 1988. The first batter he faced in the top of the first inning of his first game was future Hall of Famer Paul Molitor of the Milwaukee Brewers. Molitor homered.

Four years later, on April 10, 1992, Eiland was pitching for the San Diego Padres in the National League (with no DH). In the second inning, Eiland came to bat for the first time in his big-league career. With two outs and Jerald Clark on base, Eiland homered off Bob Ojeda of the Los Angeles Dodgers, becoming the first pitcher to 1) *surrender* a home run to the first batter he ever faced in the majors, and 2) *hit* a home run in his first big league at-bat. This was the only home run of Eiland's 10-year big-league career.

July 2, 1930

Carl Reynolds Homers in Each of the First Three Innings

Scene: Yankee Stadium, New York City
Attendance: 20,000

With two outs in the top of the first inning of Game Two of a doubleheader, twenty-seven-year-old Chicago White Sox left fielder Carl Reynolds[35] hit a ball to left field that went for an inside-the-park home run. The New York Yankees pitcher was Charles "Red" Ruffing. Chicago scored three runs in the inning, and a second inside-the-park homer was hit by John Kerr.

With two outs in the second, Reynolds homered again off Ruffing, scoring Morris "Moe" Berg[36] and Hal McKain. Babe Ruth injured himself on the play, and the White Sox scored four runs in the inning.

In the third inning—again with two outs, this time facing Ken Holloway—Reynolds hit his 3rd home run of the game, this time with McKain and Johnny Watwood on base. It was his 2nd inside-the-parker of the game. The Sox scored another four runs in this inning.

Reynolds was the first player to homer in the first, second, and third innings in one game.

Eight future Hall of Famers appeared in this game: umpire Bill McGowan, Yankees Ruffing, Babe Ruth, Lefty Gomez, Lou Gehrig, Tony Lazzeri, Bill Dickey, and Earle Combs.

Final score: Chicago 15, Yankees 4.

---

35. From LaRue, Texas.
36. That's Moe Berg, Esq. In addition to being a catcher, a spy, and a winner of the Medal of Freedom (which he turned down), Berg was an attorney. He was fluent in eight languages: English, German, French, Spanish, Latin, Greek, Italian, and Sanskrit. One of Berg's many quirks was that he refused to read a newspaper that had already been read by somebody else. He said the already-read paper was "dead." He's right!

July 2, 1941

Joe DiMaggio Breaks Willie Keeler's Consecutive-Games Hitting Record with a Home Run

Scene: Yankee Stadium, New York City
Attendance: 8,682

Nineteen forty-one was very good for Joe DiMaggio of the New York Yankees and Ted Williams of the Boston Red Sox. By the end of the season, Williams had hit .406. Nobody has hit .400 since. Joe D. hit in 56 consecutive games and was the MVP of the American League.

In this Yankees–Red Sox game on July 2, DiMaggio had only one hit—a home run in the fifth inning off Dick Newsome. That extended DiMaggio's consecutive-games hitting streak to 45 games and broke the previous record of 44 set 44 years before by Wee Willie Keeler in 1897.

Nine future Hall of Famers appeared in this game, including Boston's Williams, Bobby Doerr, Joe Cronin, and Jimmie Foxx; and the Yankees' DiMaggio, Lefty Gomez, Phil Rizzuto, Joe Gordon, and Bill Dickey.

Joe DiMaggio's younger brother Dom of the Red Sox also played in this game.

Final score: Yankees 8, Red Sox 4.

July 3, 2016

Mark Teixeira Hits His 400th Home Run

Scene: PetCo Park, San Diego
Attendance: 42,131

In the top of the eighth inning of an interleague game, switch-hitting New York Yankees first baseman Mark Teixeira homered off San Diego Padres pitcher Carlos Villanueva.

In the ninth, Teixeira homered again, this time with Brett Gardner on base. The pitcher was Kevin Quackenbush.[37]

The first of Teixeira's two home runs was the 400th of his career (2003–2016). The Yankees became the first team to boast three players who had each hit 400 home runs as of July 3: Teixeira(400), Alex Rodriguez(695), and Carlos Beltran(411).

Final score: Yankees 6, Padres 3.

July 4, 1939

George Selkirk Homers in Both Games of a Doubleheader on "Lou Gehrig Appreciation Day"

Scene:　　　Yankee Stadium, New York City
Attendance:　61,808

On "Lou Gehrig Appreciation Day," the New York Yankees played a doubleheader with the Washington Senators.

In the bottom of the ninth inning of Game One, George "Twinkletoes" Selkirk homered off Emil "Dutch" Leonard.

Final score: Senators 3, Yankees 2.

In the fourth inning of the second game, Selkirk homered again, this time off Pete Appleton (born Peter William Jablonowski).[38]

Final score: Yankees 11, Senators 1.

July 4, 2017

Aaron Judge Dents Yankee Stadium II

Scene:　　　Yankee Stadium II, New York City
Attendance:　44,018

37.　Quackenbush is the only major leaguer born in Land O'Lakes, Florida.
38.　Appleton is the only major leaguer from Terryville, Connecticut.

Aaron Judge (AP Photo/Kathy Willens)

In the bottom of the fourth inning, New York Yankees rookie right fielder Aaron Judge smashed a blast off Toronto Blue Jays pitcher J. A. Happ, which dented a metal casement above a door in left-center field, 456 feet from home plate. It was Judge's 28th home run of the season.

Final score: Blue Jays 4, Yankees 1.

July 5, 2017

Aaron Judge Ties Joe DiMaggio's Yankee Rookie Record with His 29th Home Run of the Season

Scene:　　　Yankee Stadium II, New York City
Attendance:　38,691

New York Yankees right fielder Aaron Judge led off the bottom of the fourth inning. On a 92-mph four-seam fastball from Toronto Blue Jays pitcher Marco Estrada, Judge slugged a home run 385 feet into the Yankee bullpen in center field—his 29th home run of the season. This tied the 81-year-old Yankees rookie record set in 1936 by Joe DiMaggio.

Final score: Blue Jays 7, Yankees 6.

July 6, 1933

Babe Ruth Hits the First Home Run in the First All-Star Game

Scene: Comiskey Park, Chicago
Attendance: 47,595

In the bottom of the third inning, with the American League's Charlie Gehringer on base, Babe Ruth hit a 1–1 pitch into the right–field seats, the first All-Star home run. The National League's pitcher was Bill Hallahan.

Babe Ruth

Nineteen future Hall of Famers appeared in this game: umpires Bill Klem and Bill McGowan, managers Connie Mack and John McGraw, Ruth, Frankie Frisch, Chuck Klein, Paul Waner, Chick Hafey, Bill Terry, Pie Traynor, Carl Hubbell, Gabby Hartnett, Lou Gehrig, Al Simmons, Joe Cronin, Lefty Gomez, Rick Ferrell, and Lefty Grove.

Final score: American League 4, National League 2.

July 7, 2017

Aaron Judge Sets the New York Yankees Record for Home Runs in a Season by a Rookie

Scene: Yankee Stadium, II, New York City
Attendance: 43,472

In the bottom of the fifth inning, New York Yankees right fielder Aaron Judge sent a 92.5-mph four-seam fastball from Milwaukee Brewers pitcher Josh Hader 408 feet into the windows above Monument Park in center field.

This was Judge's 30th home run of the season, breaking Joe DiMaggio's 1936 team rookie record of 29. And Judge still had more than half a season to go, ultimately finishing with 52!

Final score: Brewers 9, Yankees 4.

July 9, 2011

Derek Jeter's 3,000th Hit Is a Home Run

Scene: Yankee Stadium II, New York City
Attendance: 48,103

In the bottom of the third inning, in his 17th year with the only team he ever played for, thirty-seven-year-old Yankees captain Derek Jeter became the second player (after Wade Boggs on August 7, 1999) to homer for his 3,000th hit—a solo shot, off David Price of the Tampa Bay Rays (see cover image).

Jeter, who never played any position but shortstop in 2,747 games, finished his career in 2014 with 3,465 hits and 260 home runs.

Final score: New York 5, Tampa Bay 4.

July 11, 2006

Babe Ruth's All-Star Home Run Ball Sold at Auction

The baseball that Babe Ruth hit for a home run in the first All-Star Game at Chicago's Comiskey Park on July 6, 1933, sold at auction on this date for $805,000.

July 13, 1934

Babe Ruth Hits His 700th Home Run

Scene: Navin Field, Detroit
Attendance: 21,000

In the top of the third inning, Earle Combs was on first when New York Yankees left fielder Babe Ruth faced Detroit Tigers pitcher Tommy Bridges.[39]

Ruth blasted a ball 480 feet over the right-field wall—the 700th home run of his career.

Babe Ruth

39. Bridges is the only major leaguer born in Gordonsville, Tennessee.

Nine future Hall of Famers appeared in this game: umpire Bill McGowan, Ruth, Lou Gehrig, Bill Dickey, Goose Goslin, Hank Greenberg, Mickey Cochrane, Charlie Gehringer, and Yankees manager Joe McCarthy.

Final score: Yankees 4, Tigers 2.

July 14, 1934

Babe Ruth Hits His Final Home Run Against the Detroit Tigers

Scene: Navin Field, Detroit
Attendance: 22,500

Submarine-ball pitcher Elden Auker[40] was on the mound for the Detroit Tigers in the top of the fourth inning when New York Yankees right fielder Babe Ruth stepped up to the plate. Lefty Gomez and Robert "Red" Rolfe were on base. Ruth clouted a 3-run home run, his final homer against the Tigers.

During his 22-year (1914–1935) career, Ruth hit 123 career homers against the Tigers, more than against any other team.

Final score: Tigers 12, Yankees 11.

July 18, 1921

Babe Ruth Breaks Roger Connor's All-Time Home-Run Mark

Scene: Navin Field, Detroit
Attendance: 3,000

In the top of the eighth inning, Babe Ruth, facing Bert Cole of the Detroit Tigers, hit his 36th home run of the 1921 season.[41]

---

40. Auker is one of two major leaguers born in Norcatur, Kansas.
41. Ruth led the major leagues with a seemingly unsurpassable 59 homers in 1921.

It was also the 139th home run of his career, breaking the 21-year-old record (138) held since April 29, 1897, by Roger Connor, a future Hall of Famer.

Final score: Yankees 10, Tigers 1.

July 18, 1987

Don Mattingly Homers in His Eighth Consecutive Game

Scene: Arlington Stadium, Arlington, Texas
Attendance: 41,871

Don Mattingly of the New York Yankees led off the top of the fourth inning by homering to left-center field on a sinker

Don Mattingly

from Texas Rangers pitcher José Guzmán—the eighth consecutive game (going back to July 8) in which Mattingly had homered, tying the 31-year-old record set by Dale Long. Mattingly hit 10 home runs during this stretch: eight to right field, one to left-center, and one to center field. Final score: Rangers 7, Yankees 2.

July 20, 1965

Pitcher Mel Stottlemyre Hits an Inside-The-Park Grand Slam

Scene: Yankee Stadium, New York City
Attendance: 24,594

Mel Stottlemyre Sr.,[42] a native of Hazleton, Missouri, was an excellent pitcher who spent his entire 11-year (1964–1974) career as a starter for the New York Yankees. He was a 20-game winner in 1965, 1968, and 1969, threw 40 shutouts, and was a five-time All-Star. His career batting average was .160, but he had occasional power—14 doubles, 6 triples, and 7 career home runs.[43]

Stottlemyre pitched in three games in the 1964 World Series, which the Yankees lost to the St. Louis Cardinals, going 1–1.

On July 20, 1965, Stottlemyre started against the Boston Red Sox. The Yankees were up 2–1 in the bottom of the fifth inning. Facing Bill Monbouquette, Joe Pepitone walked, and Clete Boyer bunted safely. Then Roger Repoz walked.

---

42. Mel Stottlemyre Sr. is one of the few major-league pitchers who had two sons pitch in the majors: Todd and Mel Jr.

43. The Yankees surprised Stottlemyre, seventy-three, who served Joe Torre as Yankees pitching coach in 1996 and 1998–2000, with a plaque in Monument Park on Old Timers Day, June 25, 2015. All the other former Yankees had been introduced and ran onto the field. Stottlemyre was the last man on the bench and thought he'd been overlooked.

Stottlemyre, a righty batter, smacked the first pitch—a high fastball—460 feet to the bleacher wall in center field for an inside-the-park grand slam—the first by a pitcher since July 22, 1910 (when Charles "Deacon" Phillippe[44] did it for the Pittsburgh Pirates). There has not been another inside-the-park grand slam hit by a pitcher in the 53 years since.

Final score: Yankees 6, Red Sox 3.

July 24, 1983

The "Pine Tar" Game[45]

Scene: Yankee Stadium, New York City
Attendance: 33,944

Going into the ninth inning, the New York Yankees led the Kansas City Royals 4–3. After U L[46] Washington of the Royals singled, the new Yankees pitcher was Rich "Goose" Gossage, a future Hall of Famer. The next batter was George Brett[47]—also a future Hall of Famer. The play that followed involved two other future Hall of Famers.

With two outs, Brett homered into the right field stands, scoring Washington to make the score 5–4 Royals. After Brett crossed home plate and returned to the Royals dugout, Yankees manager Billy Martin ran out to home plate to "suggest" to rookie home-plate umpire Tim McClelland that the pine tar on Brett's bat went up too far. According to rule 1.10.c, pine tar may go up no more than 18 inches from the tip of the handle. Martin had noticed the length of the pine tar on

44. Phillippe is the only major leaguer who was born in Rural Retreat, Virginia.
45. This is one of the few major-league games named for a home run.
46. Those are not his initials. The letters don't stand for anything. His name is "U L". Washington is from Stringtown, Oklahoma.
47. Brett is the only major leaguer born in Glen Dale, West Virginia.

Brett's bat in an earlier game in Kansas City, but he bided his time: "You don't call him on it if he makes an out."

Martin, a sly baseball strategist, knew the rule well: Yankees catcher Thurman Munson had lost an RBI on July 19, 1975, when home-plate umpire Art Frantz ruled that the pine tar on *his* bat went up too high.

Not surprisingly, none of the umpires who conferred about Brett's 34½-inch bat—he later said that this was his favorite bat—was in possession of a ruler or a tape measure. But they all knew the official width of home plate—17 inches. When they laid Brett's bat across the plate, they saw that the pine tar on it exceeded the width of home plate by more than 1 inch. McClelland pointed to Brett in the dugout and called him out. Game over, Yankees win 4–3. But . . .

Brett charged out of the dugout as enraged as any major leaguer ever was: what had been a home run was now a game-losing out. Brett had to be restrained. Meanwhile, Brett's teammate Gaylord Perry—the third future Hall of Famer involved in the incident—tried to grab the bat and get it back to the Royals dugout, but he was restrained by umpire crew chief Joe Brinkman.

The Royals filed a protest and appealed to American League president Lee MacPhail (future Hall of Famer number four), who upheld the appeal. Brett eschewed batting gloves. Unlike a corked bat or a bat with nails in it, the existence of the pine tar on Brett's bat was not cheating, MacPhail ruled. Brett had not violated the "spirit of the rules" and had not deliberately "altered the bat to improve the distance factor." The home run counted, and the game would continue from that point.

Twenty-five days after the first time the game ended, on August 18, the game recommenced on what would have been an off day for both teams. This time, Yankees pitcher Ron Guidry played center field and Don Mattingly was at second. Yankees pitcher George Frazier appealed, claiming that Brett had failed to touch both first and second base. Umpire crew chief Dave Phillips had anticipated this ploy: he produced a notarized letter signed by all four umpires affirming that Brett and Washington had touched all the bases. Both runs counted. The Yankees failed to score in the bottom of the ninth. For the second time, the game was over.

Final score: Royals 5, Yankees 4.

July 26, 1939

Bill Dickey Hits Three Home Runs off Three Different Pitchers

Scene: Yankee Stadium, New York City
Attendance: 4,843[48]—*not* a typo.

In the bottom of the third inning, Yankees catcher Bill Dickey came to bat with two outs. He homered off St. Louis Browns pitcher George Gill.[49]

In the sixth, Dickey homered again with Joe DiMaggio on base and one out, this time off John Whitehead.

Dickey came to bat again in the eighth inning with no outs and nobody on base. This time, he homered off Alfred "Roxie" Lawson—for his 3rd home run, off the third different pitcher!

Final score: Yankees 14, Browns 1.

Bill Dickey

48. See entry for September 22, 1966.
49. Too bad Gill wasn't a catcher. He's a native of Catchings, Mississippi.

July 27, 1975

Alex Rodriguez Is Born

Alex Rodriguez, who hit 696 home runs during his 22-year (1994–2016) career with the Seattle Mariners (189 home runs), Texas Rangers (156 home runs), and New York Yankees (351 home runs), was born in New York City.

July 27, 1988

Jeff Leonard's Inside-the-Park, Three-Error Home Run

Scene: Yankee Stadium, New York City
Attendance: 28,869

In the top of the fourth inning, with one out and Jim Gantner on base for the Milwaukee Brewers, Jeff "Penitentiary Face" Leonard came to bat against New York Yankees pitching star Tommy John.[50]

Leonard hit the ball between first base and the pitcher's mound. John bobbled the ball for an error, then threw it past first baseman Don Mattingly and down the right-field line for a second error.

Right fielder Dave Winfield retrieved the ball (which may have hit the batboy) and threw home to get Gantner. John cut off the throw and threw wildly to the plate for error number 3. Gantner scored, and so did Leonard.

John's three errors on one play tied the record for most errors on one play by a pitcher set by James "Cy" Seymour of the New York Giants in 1898.

Final score: Yankees 16, Brewers 3.

---

50. John is one of two major-league pitchers who had a medical procedure named for him (Tommy John surgery). The other is Orel Hershiser III.

July 30, 2017

The New York Yankees Shirt That Aaron Judge Wore When He Hit His First Home Run in His First Major League At-Bat Sells at Auction for $157,366

Aaron Judge made his major league debut with the New York Yankees on August 13, 2016. He homered in his first at-bat. (See entry for August 13, 2016.)

On July 30, 2017, the Yankees shirt he wore during that at-bat, sporting number 99, sold at a Steiner Sports auction for $157,366.

July 31, 2005

Brothers Bengie and José Molina Homer in the Same Game

Scene: Yankee Stadium, New York City
Attendance: 53,653

In the top of the fourth inning, with Orlando Cabrera and Juan Rivera on base, catcher Bengie Molina of the Anaheim Angels homered off New York Yankees pitcher Randy Johnson.

In the fifth inning, Molina's younger brother José, playing first base, blasted a solo home run, also off Johnson.

Final score: Yankees 8, Angels 7.

AUGUST

August 6, 1979

Bobby Murcer Hits a Home Run for Thurman Munson

Scene: Yankee Stadium, New York City
Attendance: 36,314

Following the tragic death of New York Yankees catcher and team captain Thurman Munson in a Cessna Citation jet crash in Summit County, Ohio, on August 2, 1979, the entire Yankee team flew to Canton for his funeral on August 6.

But they also had a game to play that night. In that game, Munson's best friend on the team, Bobby Murcer, who had delivered

Bobby Murcer

a tear-filled eulogy a few hours earlier, came to bat in the bottom of the seventh inning, facing "El Presidente," Dennis Martínez of the Baltimore Orioles.

Murcer homered into the right-field seats—his first home run after being reacquired by the Yankees in June. Murcer ultimately drove in all of the Yankees' 5 runs that day.

Murcer later gave the bat with which he hit the home run to Munson's widow, Diana.

Final score: Yankees 5, Orioles 4.

August 11, 1929

Babe Ruth Hits Home Run Number 500

Scene: League Park, Cleveland
Attendance: 25,000

In the top of the second inning, Babe Ruth of the Yankees hit the first pitch from Willis Hudlin[51] of the Cleveland Indians—a high fastball—over the right-field fence for his 30th home run of the season and the 500th home run of his career.

Ruth was the first player ever to hit 500 home runs. At the time, his total was *more than twice that of any other player.* The closest to Ruth at the time was Fred "Cy" Williams[52] of the Philadelphia Phillies, who had 234.

After it bounced onto Lexington Avenue adjacent to the ballpark, the ball was retrieved by Jake Geiser, a passerby. Geiser returned it to Ruth in exchange for two autographed baseballs and an autographed $20 bill.[53]

Nine future Hall of Famers participated in this game: umpire Bill McGowan, Yankees manager Miller Huggins, Ruth, Earle Combs, Lou Gehrig, Bill Dickey, Tony Lazzeri, Joe Sewell, and Earl Averill Sr.

Final score: Indians 6, Yankees 5.

August 13, 2016

Tyler Austin and Aaron Judge Hit Back-to-Back Home Runs in Their First Big League At-Bats

Scene: Yankee Stadium II, New York City
Attendance: 41,682

---

51. Hudlin is from Wagoner, Oklahoma.
52. Williams is a native of Wadena, Indiana.
53. Compare the entry for February 4, 2010.

In the bottom of the second inning, twenty-four-year-old first baseman Christopher "Tyler" Austin made his memorable big-league debut with the New York Yankees. Facing Matt Andriese of the Tampa Bay Rays in his first at-bat, with two strikes, Austin homered over the 314-foot sign in right field. Exciting enough, right? Wrong.

The very next batter, wearing number 99, was twenty-four-year-old right fielder Aaron Judge,[54] making *his* big-league debut too. Judge homered over the 408-foot sign in center field—the first teammates to hit back-to-back home runs in their first at-bats.

Final score: Yankees 8, Tampa Bay 4.

August 16, 1927

Babe Ruth Hits a Ball Out of Comiskey Park

Scene: Comiskey Park, Chicago
Attendance: 20,000

In the top of the fifth inning, New York Yankees slugger Babe Ruth homered off Chicago White Sox pitcher Alphonse "Tommy" Thomas—the first home run ever hit over the roof at Comiskey Park.

Final score: Yankees 8, White Sox 1.

Babe Ruth

August 17, 1948

Tommy Henrich Hits His 4th Grand Slam of the Season

Scene: Griffith Stadium, Washington, D.C.
Attendance: 24,000

---

54. At 6'7" and 285 pounds, Judge is one of the largest, most intimidating players in the game. He's the only major leaguer from Linden, California, 2010 population 1,784.

In the top of the third inning, New York Yankees first baseman Tommy Henrich homered off Washington Senators pitcher Sid Hudson[55] with Bob Porterfield, Snuffy Stirnweiss, and Bobby Brown aboard.

This was Henrich's 4th grand slam of the season, tying a record (since broken) set by Babe Ruth in 1929.

Final score: Yankees 8, Senators 1.

August 21, 1931

Babe Ruth Hits Home Run Number 600

Scene: Sportsman's Park, St. Louis
Attendance: 7,500

In the top of the third inning, New York Yankees left fielder Babe Ruth hit his 35th home run of the season—a 2-run blast off George Blaeholder of the St. Louis Browns. Ruth finished the season with 46 home runs, tops in the majors.

This was Ruth's 600th career round-tripper. The ball hit a car on Grand Boulevard outside the ballpark and was retrieved by young Tony Gallico, who exchanged it with Ruth for $10 and a new ball.

The next batter, Lou Gehrig, also homered to Grand Boulevard, his 34th long blast of the season.

In the seventh inning, third-base umpire Roy Van Graflan ejected Ruth for arguing that a ball hit by Ralph "Red" Kress of the Browns that hit the top of the grandstand wall should have been a double, rather than a home run.

Ten future Hall of Famers appeared in this game: Ruth, Gehrig, Bill Dickey, Tony Lazzeri, Earle Combs, Red Ruffing, and Joe Sewell of the Yankees, plus Goose Goslin and

---

55. Hudson is a native of Coalfield, Tennessee.

Rick Ferrell of the Browns. Joe McCarthy managed the Yankees.

Final score: Yankees 11, Browns 7.

August 23, 1942

Babe Ruth, 47, Homers off Walter Johnson, 54, in an Exhibition Game

Before a sold-out crowd of 69,136 at Yankee Stadium, an exhibition was staged to raise money for the Army-Navy Service Fund[56] between games of a doubleheader between the Washington Senators and the New York Yankees[57]. Future Hall of Fame umpire Billy Evans was behind the plate. The catcher was Benny Bengough. On the mound was fifty-four-year-old Hall of Fame pitcher Walter Johnson, 15 years after his retirement. In the batter's box was forty-seven-year-old Hall of Famer Babe Ruth, seven years after his final game.

After flailing at a few pitches, Ruth gave the crowd what they wanted to see: a home run into the right-field stands of "Ruthville."

August 24, 2007

A Late Home Run

Scene: Comerica Park, Detroit
Attendance: 44,163—at the *beginning* of the game

It rained in Detroit as the New York Yankees visited the Tigers. The start of their game was delayed by four hours and one minute—longer than most games take.

---

56. Over $80,000 was raised.
57. The second game was called due to darkness and wartime restrictions on lights after the top of the sixth inning with the Yankees leading 3–0.

By the end of five innings, the game was tied at 6. It was still tied at six in the bottom of the 11th inning when Tigers shortstop Carlos Guillén faced Yankees pitcher Sean Henn with Sean Casey and Magglio Ordóñez on base at *3:30 in the morning*. Guillen ended the game with a 3-run walk-off home run. Final score: Tigers 9, Yankees 6.

August 25, 2011

The New York Yankees Hit a Record Three Grand Slams in One Game

Scene: Yankee Stadium II, New York City
Attendance: 46,369

In the bottom of the fifth inning, Yankees second baseman Robinson Cano[58] hit a grand slam off Rich Harden of the Oakland Athletics, scoring Derek Jeter, Curtis Granderson, and Alex Rodriguez.

Yankees catcher Russell Martin hit a solo home run in the fourth inning. He came to bat again in the sixth with Granderson, Rodriguez, and Nick Swisher on base. Martin hit a grand slam off pitcher Fautino De Los Santos—the fourth time the Yankees had hit 2 grand slams in a game, and the first time since 1999.

And as they say in infomercials, *But wait! There's more!*

In the eighth inning, Granderson hit a 1–2 Bruce Billings pitch for a grand slam over the right-field fence, scoring Martin, Eduardo Núñez, and Brett Gardner—the first time (and only, as of the 2017 season) any team had hit 3 grand slams in one game.

---

58. Cano was named for Jackie Robinson.

Jorge Posada played second base late in the game. The Yankees had 17 bases-loaded at-bats.

Final score: The Yankees, who had been down 7–1 early in the game, won: 22–9.

This game took four hours and 31 minutes. The start was delayed by rain for 90 minutes.

August 27, 1909

Ty Cobb and Sam Crawford Hit Back-to-Back Inside-the-Park Home Runs

Scene: Bennett Park, Detroit

Facing New York Yankees pitcher "Happy" Jack Chesbro in the bottom of the fourth inning, Detroit Tigers Ty Cobb and Sam Crawford hit back-to-back inside-the-park home runs— so far, the only future Hall of Famers to accomplish this feat.

Final score: Tigers 17, Yankees 6.

SEPTEMBER

DID YOU KNOW?

Lou Gehrig hit the most World Series home runs in his hometown: 5. Gehrig, a native New Yorker, homered in Game Two of the 1928 World Series at Yankee Stadium. In Game One of the 1932 Series, he homered again at Yankee Stadium. In the 1936 Series, Gehrig homered in Games Three and Four, both at Yankee Stadium. In the 1937 Series, he homered in Game Four, played at the Polo Grounds, home of the New York Giants. Gehrig hit 5 other World Series home runs, for a total of 10.

September 3, 1961

The First Teammates to Hit 50 Home Runs Each in a Season: Mickey Mantle and Roger Maris

Scene: Yankee Stadium, New York City
Attendance: 55,676

In the bottom of the first inning, New York Yankees center fielder Mickey Mantle homered off Jim Bunning of the Detroit Tigers with Roger Maris on base. In the ninth, Mantle homered again, this time off Gerry Staley.

The homer off Staley was Mantle's 50th home run of the season. He joined Maris, who hit his 50th homer of the season on August 22, as the first teammates each to hit 50 home runs in a single season. Mantle finished the season with 54. Maris hit a record 61.

Final score: Yankees 8, Tigers 5.

September 4, 2017

Didi Gregorius Does Something No Other Yankee Shortstop Has Ever Done

Scene: Orioles Park at Camden Yards, Baltimore
Attendance: 37,622

In the top of the fourth inning, Yankees shortstop Didi Gregorius[59] faced Baltimore Orioles pitcher Dylan Bundy with Starlin Castro on base. With the count 1–2, Gregorius

---

59. Gregorius, whose given first name is Mariekson, is one of only eight big-leaguers born in the Netherlands, and one of only two born in Amsterdam. Baseball is in his blood. His mother, Sheritsa Stroop, pitched for the Dutch national softball team. His father Johannes was a pitcher. Didi's paternal grandfather Antonio was one of the greatest pitchers in Curaçao. Didi and his family moved to Curaçao when he

smashed an 82-mph slider for a line-drive homer off the scoreboard in right field—his 20th home run of the season.

Gregorius is the first shortstop in Yankees history to have back-to-back seasons with 20 home runs. In 2016, he scorched 20 round-trippers for New York.

Final score: Yankees 7, Orioles 4.

September 5, 1989

Deion Sanders Homers for the New York Yankees

Scene: The Kingdome, Seattle
Attendance: 14,905

In the fourth inning, with Mike Blowers on base, Yankees left fielder "Neon" Deion Sanders socked a homer off Jerry Reed of the Seattle Mariners.

Final score: Yankees 12, Mariners 2. So?

Five days later, on September 10, playing for the Atlanta Falcons against the Los Angeles Rams in his first National Football League game, Sanders returned a punt 68 yards for a touchdown—the first player to hit a major league home run and score a touchdown in the NFL *in the same month*.

Final score: Rams 31, Falcons 21.

September 7, 1952

Johnny Mize Hits a Pinch-Hit Grand Slam

Scene: Griffith Stadium, Washington, D.C.
Attendance: 19,521

---

was five. He speaks English, Spanish, Dutch, and Papiamento, the language of Curaçao, Aruba, and Bonaire.

The Washington Senators were leading the Yankees 1–0 in the top of the sixth inning when Johnny Mize of the Yankees pinch-hit for Gil McDougald. With the bases loaded (Billy Martin, Phil Rizzuto, "Steady" Eddie Lopat), Mize faced Senators pitcher Walt Masterson. Mize delivered a pinch-hit grand slam. Mize had now homered in all 15 major league ballparks.[60] Final score: Yankees 5, Senators 1.

September 7, 2012

Alex Rodriguez Hits His 300th Home Run as a New York Yankee

Scene: Oriole Park at Camden Yards, Baltimore
Attendance   40,861

In the top of the fifth inning, New York Yankees third baseman Alex Rodriguez came to bat with two outs and Derek Jeter on base. The pitcher was Wei-Yin Chen[61] of the Baltimore Orioles. Rodriguez smashed his 16th homer of the season.

This was also Rodriguez's 300th home run as a Yankee, joining Babe Ruth, Lou Gehrig, Joe DiMaggio, Mickey Mantle, and Yogi Berra—all Hall of Famers—as the only players who had hit 300 homers as Yankees. The Yankees were the first team for which six players had hit 300 home runs.

Final score: Yankees 8, Orioles 5.

---

60. Sixteen teams, 15 parks—the St. Louis Cardinals shared Busch Stadium with the St. Louis Browns from 1920 to 1953.
61. Chen is the first major leaguer from Kaohsiung City, Taiwan.

September 8, 1916

Wally Schang Switch-Hits Home Runs

Scene: Shibe Park, Philadelphia
Attendance: 23—the smallest "crowd" in American League history.[62]

In the bottom of the first inning, Philadelphia Athletics Whitey Witt, Otis Lawry, and Jim Brown were on base when catcher Wally Schang, batting lefty, hit a grand slam over the wall in right field off New York Yankees pitcher Allen Russell.

In the second, Shang, batting righty, connected for a solo shot off Edward "Slim" Love[63] that went through the scoreboard.

Schang was the first American Leaguer to switch-hit home runs in the same game.

Final score: A's 8, Yankees 2.

September 9, 1936

Lou Gehrig Hits His 13th Home Run of the Season Against the Cleveland Indians

Scene: Cleveland Stadium
Attendance: 10,000

Doubleheader, Game Two—in the top of the second inning, the Yankees had the bases loaded with Irving "Bump" Hadley, Frank Crosetti, and Joe DiMaggio when first baseman Lou Gehrig came to bat. Oral Hildebrand of the Indians was on the mound.

---

62. That's except for the game the Orioles hosted in Baltimore on April 29, 2015, which, because of riots in the city, had *no* fans in the stands.
63. Slim Love is the only major league ballplayer born in Love, Mississippi. What are the odds?

Gehrig hit a grand slam—his 13th home run of the season—against the Indians. He hit his 14th against the Indians the next day.

Final score: Yankees 12, Indians 9.

September 10, 2017

Aaron Judge Sets a Record

Scene: Globe Life Park, Arlington, Texas
Attendance: 31,349

New York Yankees right fielder Aaron Judge set a record on this date, but it had nothing to do with the 2 home runs he hit in the game, his 40th and 41st of the season.[64]

The only other Yankees to hit 40 home runs in a season before their 25th birthday are Babe Ruth (1920), Lou Gehrig (1927), Joe DiMaggio (1936), and Mickey Mantle (1956).

Judge was walked in the top of the second inning by Texas Rangers pitcher A. J. Griffin—Judge's 107th walk of the season, breaking the rookie record for walks in a season set by Ted Williams on September 30, 1939, in the final game of the year against the Yankees.

Final score: Yankees 16, Rangers 7.

September 11, 1966

John Miller Homers in His First Plate Appearance

Scene: Fenway Park, Boston
Attendance: 15,482

---

64. Judge's first home run to right-center field, on a 3–2 fastball from Rangers pitcher Yohander Mendez in the sixth inning, made Judge just the second rookie to hit at least 40 home run in a season. The first was Mark McGwire of the Oakland A's, who hit 49 in 1987.

With Joe Pepitone on base in the top of the second inning, twenty-two-year-old Yankees left fielder John Miller homered in his first big-league plate appearance off Boston Red Sox pitcher Albert Lee "Stinger" Stange.

Miller hit his second and final home run in his last big-league at-bat in the first game of a doubleheader on September 23, 1969, when he was with the Los Angeles Dodgers.

Miller was the first player to homer in his first and last at-bat.

Final score: Yankees 4, Red Sox 2.

September 13, 1936

Joe DiMaggio Hits His 29th Home Run of His Rookie Season

Scene: Sportsman's Park, St. Louis
Attendance: 8,000

Doubleheader, Game Two—in the top of the seventh inning, Yankees rookie center fielder Joe DiMaggio, 21 years old, faced St. Louis Browns pitcher Ivy Andrews.[65] DiMaggio slugged his 29th home run of the season.

Final score: Yankees 13, Browns 1 in one hour, 49 minutes. The Yankees starting nine played the entire game.

DiMaggio's mark of 29 home runs in a season stood as the Yankees' rookie record until it was broken by Aaron Judge 81 years later, on July 7, 2017.

---

65. Andrews is the only big leaguer from Dora, Alabama.

September 15, 1950

Johnny Mize Hits 3 Home Runs in One Game for a Record Fourth Time

Scene: Briggs Stadium, Detroit
Attendance: 23,900

"Big Jawn" Johnny Mize of the Yankees homered in the first, fourth, and fifth innings, each time off Art Houtteman of the Detroit Tigers.

This marked the record fourth time that Mize had connected for 3 home runs in one game.

The first three times Mize hit 3 homers in a game were on July 20, 1938, May 13, 1940, and September 8, 1940—all when he was a St. Louis Cardinal.

Final score: Tigers 9, Yankees 7.

September 16, 1940

Johnny Lucadello—The First Player to Switch-Hit His First Two Home Runs in One Game

Scene: Sportsman's Park, St. Louis
Attendance: 1,343

In the bottom of the first inning, second baseman Johnny Lucadello[66] of the St. Louis Browns, batting righty, hit the

---

66. Lucadello, the only native of Thurber, Texas, to play in the majors, was signed to his first pro contract by his brother Tony. Johnny Lucadello was a minor-league All-Star. He spent four years (1942–1945) in the

first home run of his career off Yankees pitcher Marius Russo, a Brooklyn native.

In the seventh inning, batting lefty, Lucadello homered again, this time off Steve Sundra.[67]

Lucadello is the first player whose first 2 career home runs were switch-hit in the same game.

Final score: Browns 16, Yankees 4.

September 17, 1938

Hank Greenberg Sets the Single-Season Record with His 11th Home Run Against New York Yankee Pitchers

Scene: Briggs Stadium, Detroit
Attendance: 19,200

With Charlie Gehringer on base in the bottom of the first inning, Detroit Tigers first baseman Hank Greenberg, a native of New York City, homered off Yankees pitcher Monte Pearson.

With Gehringer and Fred "Dixie" Walker[68] on base in the fifth, Greenberg blasted his 2nd round tripper of the day off Pearson.

Greenberg's second homer was his 11th off Yankees pitching in 1938. Seventy-nine years later, that's still the record for most home runs against the Yankees in a single season.

The game was played in one hour and 50 minutes, with no relief pitchers, no pinch-hitters, and no pinch-runners.

Final score: Tigers 7, Yankees 3.

U.S. Navy at the Great Lakes Naval Training Center near Chicago, in Hawaii, at the Marshall Islands, and in Tinian before his discharge. He hit .264 and hit 5 homers during his six-year (1938–1941, 1946–1947) big-league career with the Browns and Yankees.

67.   Sundra is the only big leaguer from Luxor, Pennsylvania.

68.   Walker is the only major leaguer from Villa Rica, Georgia.

Nine future Hall of Famers were on the field for this game: umpire Bill McGowan, Greenberg, Charlie Gehringer, Red Rolfe, Joe DiMaggio, Lou Gehrig, Bill Dickey, and Joe Gordon. The Yankees manager was Joe McCarthy.

September 17, 1977

Dave Kingman Homers for His Fourth Team of the Season

Scene: Tiger Stadium, Detroit
Attendance: 17,656

In 1977, Dave Kingman hit 9 home runs for the New York Mets (National League East), 11 for the San Diego Padres (National League West), and 2 for the California Angels (American League West).

On September 17, 1977, Kingman hit his 1st home run for the Yankees of the American League East. The blow came in the top of the third inning, with Lou Piniella on base and Jim Crawford on the mound for the Detroit Tigers. Kingman had gone deep for teams in all four divisions in one season.

Final score: Yankees 9, Tigers 4.

September 19, 1937

Hank Greenberg: First Player to Hit a Home Run into the Center-Field Bleachers at Yankee Stadium

Scene: Yankee Stadium, New York City
Attendance: 17,420

With two outs in the top of the seventh inning, Detroit Tigers first baseman Hank Greenberg, a New York City native, blasted a two-out pitch from Yankee Irving "Bump" Hadley about 425 feet into the center-field bleachers at Yankee Stadium—the first player to hit one there.

The bleachers were later replaced with a black batter's-eye section.

Final score: Tigers 8, Yankees 1.

September 19, 1968

Denny McLain Grooves a Pitch to Mickey Mantle. He Clobbers It.

Scene: Tiger Stadium, Detroit
Attendance 9,063

The 1968 baseball season was almost over. Pitcher Denny McLain of the Detroit Tigers had already won 30 games—the last pitcher to do so. Mickey Mantle of the Yankees would retire at the end of the season. At the time he had hit 534 home runs, tied with Jimmie Foxx.[69]

Catcher Jim Price and McLain agreed to give the fans a big thrill by letting Mantle hit another home run. Price mentioned it to Mantle, who saw McClain nod in agreement.

With one out in the top of the eighth inning, with the Tigers leading 6–1, Mantle got the pitch he wanted—not too fast, high, and inside. He smashed it to the upper deck in right field, breaking his tie with Foxx. It was the next-to-last homer of Mantle's career. As he crossed home plate, he thanked Price.

Final score: Tigers 6, Yankees 2.

September 20, 1968

Mickey Mantle's Final Home Run

Scene: Yankee Stadium, New York City
Attendance: 15,737

---

69. Foxx is now number 19 on the all-time home run list. Mantle is number 18 with 536.

Mickey Mantle

With two outs in the bottom of the third inning, Mickey Mantle of the Yankees, then 36 and playing first base, homered off Boston Red Sox pitcher Jim Lonborg. It was home run number 536 for Mantle—the last one of his stellar 18-year (1951–1968) career, all with the Yankees.

When he retired, Mantle was number 2 on the all-time home-run list. Only Babe Ruth had more—714. As of 2017, Mantle is number 18.

Final score: Boston 4, New York 3.

September 20, 2013

Alex Rodriguez Breaks Lou Gehrig's Record of 23 Career Grand Slams

Scene: Yankee Stadium II, New York City
Attendance: 41,734

In the bottom of the seventh inning, thirty-eight-year-old Yankees designated hitter Alex Rodriguez, a New York City native, came to bat against San Francisco Giants reliever George Kontos. With two outs and the game tied at one, the bases were loaded with Brendan Ryan, John Ryan Murphy, and Ichiro Suzuki. On a 2–1 pitch, Rodriguez homered to right field—his 24th career grand slam, eclipsing the record of 23 career grand slams set by fellow Yankee and New York City native Lou Gehrig 75 years before on August 20, 1938.

Final score: Yankees 5, Giants 1.

September 20, 2017

Didi Gregorius Set the Record for Most Home Runs in a Season by a Yankees Shortstop

Scene: Yankee Stadium II, New York City
Attendance: 30,099

In the bottom of the fourth inning, Yankees shortstop Didi Gregorius came to bat with Gary Sanchez and Brett Gardner on base. The pitcher was Tyler Duffey of the Minnesota Twins.

Gregorius smashed a 90-mph two-seam fastball into the stands in right-center field for his 25th home run of the season, breaking a tie with Derek Jeter to become the record-holder for most home runs in a season by a Yankees shortstop.

Final score: Yankees 11, Twins 3.

September 21, 2008

Last Game Ever at Yankee Stadium

Scene: Yankee Stadium, New York City
Attendance: 54,610

The New York Yankees were stuck in a disappointing third place for their final home game of the 2008 season, but the stadium was sold out. It was the last game *ever* at Yankee Stadium, to be replaced by a new Yankee Stadium in 2009.

The ceremonial first pitch was thrown out by ninety-two-year-old Julia Ruth Stevens, Babe Ruth's daughter.

With Robinson Cano on base in the bottom of the fourth inning and Chris Waters on the mound for the Baltimore Orioles, Yankees catcher José Molina hit the 11,270th and final home run at Yankee Stadium.

Final score: Yankees 7, Orioles 3.

September 22, 1946

Yogi Berra Homers in His First Big League Game

Scene: Yankee Stadium, New York City
Attendance: 24,951

Yogi Berra

Doubleheader, Game One—with Charlie Keller on base in the bottom of the fourth inning, Lawrence Peter "Yogi" Berra came to bat for the second time in the first game of his major-league career. He smacked a home run off Philadelphia Athletics pitcher Jesse Flores, the first of 358 he hit in his 19-year (1946–1963, 1965) Hall of Fame career.

Final score: Yankees 4, Athletics 3.

September 22, 1966

Tommie Agee and Tom McCraw Homer

Scene: Yankee Stadium, New York City
Attendance: 413-not a typographical error.

The season was almost over, and the Yankees would finish in an unaccustomed last place, 70–89, 26½ games behind the first-place Baltimore Orioles.

In the top of the ninth inning, Chicago White Sox center fielder Tommie Agee[70] hit an inside-the-park home run off Horace "Dooley" Womack. The next batter, Tommy McCraw, also homered, to complete the set of back-to-back home runs, including an inside-the-parker, in front of a group of only 413 fans (66,587 empty seats).

"The Ol' Redhead" Red Barber[71] lost his job as the Yankees television broadcaster after he asked for, but didn't get, a camera shot of the empty stands. He told the audience: "I don't know what the paid attendance is today, but whatever

---

70. Agee is a native of Magnolia, Alabama.
71. Barber is one of the first two winners, along with Mel Allen, of the Ford C. Frick Award for broadcasting at the National Baseball Hall of Fame (1978), and winner of a Peabody Award for excellence in broadcasting.

it is, it is the smallest crowd in the history of Yankee Stadium, and this crowd is the story, not the game."

Final score: White Sox 4, Yankees 1.

September 23, 1933

Tom Oliver Does Not Hit a Home Run

Scene: Fenway Park, Boston
Attendance: 4,000

With the New York Yankees ahead 16–12, Tom "Rebel" Oliver of the Boston Red Sox pinch-hit for Allen "Dusty" Cooke[72] in the bottom of the ninth inning against Yankees pitcher Russ Van Atta. Oliver struck out.

It was the final major-league at-bat for Oliver, an outfielder. In his 2,073 plate appearances over four seasons (1930–1933), he had 0 home runs—a record at the time.

Final score: Yankees 16, Red Sox 12.

September 24, 1919

Babe Ruth Breaks the Single-Season Home Run Record

Scene: The Polo Grounds, New York City
Attendance: 7,500

In the top of the ninth inning of Game Two of a doubleheader, Boston Red Sox left fielder Babe Ruth blasts one over the roof for his 28th home run of the season. The Yankees pitcher was Bob Shawkey.[73]

---

72. From Swepsonville, North Carolina.
73. Shawkey is the only major leaguer from Sigel, Pennsylvania.

This breaks the record for home runs in a season previously held by Ned Williamson of the Chicago White Stockings (later the Cubs) in the National League, set on October 11, 1884.

Final score: Yankees 2, Red Sox 1.

September 25, 2017

Aaron Judge Breaks the Record for Home Runs in a Season by a Rookie

Scene: Yankee Stadium II, New York City
Attendance: 40,023

In the bottom of the third inning of a make-up game, Brett Gardner was on base when Yankees rookie right fielder Aaron Judge came to bat facing Kansas City Royals pitcher Jakob Junis.[74] Judge hit his 49th home run of the season, a mighty blast into the right-field seats, tying the record Oakland A's first baseman Mark McGwire set on September 29, 1987, for most home runs in a season by a rookie.

McGwire might have hit more that season, but he left the team to be with his wife, who was in labor.

In the seventh inning, facing Trevor Cahill, Judge connected again for his record 50th blast of the season, a long shot to the left-field seats.

Final score: Yankees 11, Royals 3.

September 27, 1923

Lou Gehrig Hits His First Home Run

Scene: Fenway Park, Boston
Attendance: 3,000

---

74. Junis is one of only three players born in Sterling, Illinois—2016 population 14,000.

Lou Gehrig

In the top of the first inning of a game that took one hour and 27 minutes, with Babe Ruth on third base, Yankees first baseman Lou Gehrig hit the first of his 493 career home runs. The pitcher was Bill Piercy of the Boston Red Sox.

Final score: Yankees 8, Red Sox 3.

September 27, 1938

Lou Gehrig Hits His Final Home Run at Yankee Stadium

Scene: Yankee Stadium, New York City
Attendance: 2,773 (The Yankees had already won the pennant.)

In the bottom of the fifth inning, Yankees first baseman Lou Gehrig came to bat with the bases empty. The pitcher was Emil "Dutch" Leonard[75] of the Washington Senators. Gehrig

---

75. Leonard is the only major leaguer from Auburn, Illinois.

homered—his 29th clout of the season and his 251st and final regular-season home run at home at Yankee Stadium.

Final Score: Yankees 5, Senators 2. The Senators used three pitchers. The Yankees played the entire game, which took only 92 minutes, with just their starting nine.

Seven future Hall of Famers were on the field for this game: Yankees manager Joe McCarthy, Senators manager Stanley "Bucky" Harris, Gehrig, Joe Gordon, Joe DiMaggio, Lefty Gomez, and Al Simmons.

After 79 years, Gehrig still holds the record for most career regular-season home runs hit by a player in his hometown—251. Gehrig is a New York City native.

September 27, 1998

Shane Spencer Hits His Third Grand Slam in September

Scene: Yankee Stadium, New York City
Attendance: 49,608

Twenty-six-year-old outfielder Michael "Shane" Spencer broke into the major leagues with the New York Yankees on April 10, 1998.

He hit a grand slam in the ninth inning on September 18, 1998, in Baltimore. Jorge Posada, Scott Brosius, and Chuck Knoblauch were on base. The pitcher was Jesse Orosco of the Orioles.

Grand slam number 2 of the month was hit in the sixth inning on September 24 at Yankee Stadium. Derek Jeter, Bernie Williams, and Homer Bush were on base. Wilson Alvarez of the Tampa Bay Devil Rays was on the mound.

On September 27, the final day of the season, at Yankee Stadium, Spencer connected in the fifth inning for his 3rd grand slam of the month, a monster blast off Albie Lopez, one of eight Tampa Bay pitchers. Williams, Luis Sojo, and Charles "Chili" Davis scored.

Final score: Yankees 8, Devil Rays 3.

Spencer finished the season with 10 homers and hit 59 during his seven-year (1998–2004) career.

September 28, 1947

Earle Combs Homers in the First Old-Timers Game

Scene: Yankee Stadium, New York City
Attendance: 23,085

Before the final home game of the 1947 season, the New York Yankees—who had already won the American League pennant—staged the first Old-Timers Day. Those on the field included Hall of Famers Cy Young, Ty Cobb, Jimmie Foxx, Lefty Gomez, Al Simmons, Frank "Home Run" Baker, Earle Combs, Tris Speaker, Harry Hooper, Waite Hoyt, Chief Bender, Urban "Red" Faber, and, of course, Babe Ruth (although he was not in uniform).

The day, which included a two-inning game in which Joe McCarthy managed the former Yankees and Connie Mack ("The Tall Tactician") managed the opponents, was a fundraiser for the Babe Ruth Foundation Fund.

Earle Combs hit a 3-run inside-the-park home run that went over the head of Tris Speaker—"The Gray Eagle." At the time, Speaker was over sixty.

September 28, 1955

Elston Howard Homers in the World Series

Scene: Yankee Stadium, New York City
Attendance: 63,869

It was Game One of the 1955 World Series, and the Brooklyn Dodgers were playing the New York Yankees for the sixth time. Before the game started, the crowd—including New York Governor W. Averell Harriman and New York City Mayor Robert Wagner—joined in a silent prayer for the quick and complete recovery of President Dwight D. Eisenhower, who had recently suffered a heart attack.

In the bottom of the second inning, Joe Collins of the Yankees was on base when twenty-six-year-old left fielder Elston Howard came to bat—his first World Series at-bat—to face Dodgers pitcher Don Newcombe, a 20-game winner during the regular season.

Howard hit a smash to the lower left-field seats—the first black man to hit a home run off a black pitcher in the World Series.

Final score: Yankees 6, Dodgers 5.

September 28, 1976

Thurman Munson Hits His Final Home Run of the 1976 Season

Scene: Fenway Park, Boston
Attendance: 21,200

In 1970, Yankees catcher Thurman Munson was named the American League Rookie of the Year. He hit .302 with 6 home runs and 53 runs batted in. He was just 23.

Thurman Munson

On this date, in the top of the third inning, Munson faced Boston Red Sox pitcher Rick Kreuger. He hit a solo home run, his 17th and last of the season.

Munson led the Yankees to the American League pennant. He batted .302 and had a career-high 105 RBIs.

Munson was named the Most Valuable Player in the American League—through 2017, still the only Yankee to have been both Rookie of the Year and later MVP.

Final score: Red Sox 7, Yankees 5.

September 30, 1927

Babe Ruth Hits His 60th Home Run of the Season

Scene: Yankee Stadium, New York City
Attendance: 8,000

This Yankees–Senators game was memorable for at least two reasons. The second is that after 21 years, 802 games, 417 wins, and 3,509 strikeouts—all with the Washington Senators—this was Walter Johnson's final game.[76] He pinch-hit for Tom Zachary in the ninth inning.

Yankees slugger George Herman "Babe" Ruth already held the record for most home runs in a single season—59, a record he set in 1921. That record seemed insurmountable. No one could *ever* break it. It would last *forever*.

Or at least for six years. The 1927 New York Yankees were an extraordinary group of ballplayers. They won 110 games. They included seven future Hall of Famers: manager Miller Huggins plus Ruth, Lou Gehrig, Tony Lazzeri, Earle Combs, Waite Hoyt, and Herb Pennock.

On September 30, 1927, the next-to-last game of the season, the game was tied at 2 going into the eighth inning. With one out and Mark Koenig on third, Ruth did the unthinkable: he hit a low inside fastball from Zachary into the right-field bleachers, his 60th home run of the season—a record that would last 34 years, until broken by Roger Maris—another Yankees outfielder—in 1961.

Final score: Yankees 4, Senators 2.

September 30, 1934
Lou Gehrig Wins the Triple Crown

Scene: Griffith Stadium, Washington, D.C.
Attendance: 15,000

In the top of the second inning of a game that took only 80 minutes, Yankees first baseman Lou Gehrig homered off Washington Senators pitcher Orville Armbrust.[77]

---

76. But see the entry for August 23, 1942.
77. Armbrust is the only big leaguer from Beirne, Arkansas.

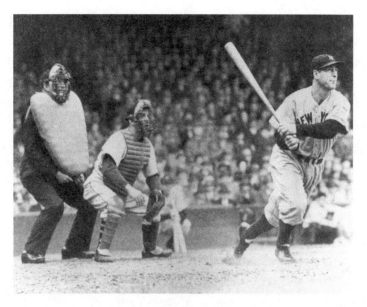

Lou Gehrig

This was Gehrig's 49th and final home run of the season. He won not only the American League home-run crown but also the Triple Crown, as he led the league with 166 RBIs and a .363 batting average. Gehrig, a native New Yorker, is the only man to win the Triple Crown playing in his home town.

Final score: Senators 5, Yankees 3. This was Armbrust's only win in his three-game career.

September 30, 1936

George Selkirk—The First Foreign-Born Player to Homer in the World Series

Scene: The Polo Grounds, New York City
Attendance: 39,419

George "Twinkletoes" Selkirk, a native of Huntsville, Ontario, Canada, led off the top of the third inning for the New York Yankees in Game One of the 1936 World Series with a home run off New York Giants pitcher Carl Hubbell—the 1st World Series home run by a foreign-born player.

Final score: Giants 6, Yankees 1.

September 30, 1953

It's a Pinch-Hit Homer in the World Series for George Shuba

Scene: Yankee Stadium, New York City
Attendance: 69,734

In the top of the sixth inning of Game One of the World Series, George "Shotgun" Shuba of the Brooklyn Dodgers pinch-hit for pitcher Jim Hughes. With Billy Cox on base, Shuba faced Yankees pitcher Allie Reynolds.

Shuba's home run was the 1st pinch-hit homer in the World Series by a National Leaguer. Shuba is just the third player after American Leaguers Yogi Berra and Johnny Mize (both Yankees) to hit a pinch-hit home run in the Fall Classic.

Eight future Hall of Famers appeared in this game: Yankees manager Casey Stengel, Pee Wee Reese, Duke Snider, Roy Campanella, Mickey Mantle, Phil Rizzuto, Yogi Berra, and Jackie Robinson.

Final score: Yankees 9, Dodgers 5.

September 30, 1962

Mickey Mantle Blasts His 30th Home Run of the Season

Scene: Yankee Stadium, New York City
Attendance: 14,685

On the final day of the season, the pennant-winning New York Yankees faced the Chicago White Sox.

Yankees centerfielder Mickey Mantle batted leadoff. With two outs in the bottom of the fourth inning, Mantle, batting lefty, faced pitcher Ray Herbert. Mantle's home run marked the seventh consecutive season he had hit at least 30 round-trippers.

Final score: White Sox 8, Yankees 4.

September 30, 2004

Bernie Williams's Home Run Wins the American League East for the New York Yankees

Scene: Yankee Stadium, New York City
Attendance: 48,454

The New York Yankees and the Minnesota Twins were tied at 4 going into the bottom of the ninth inning. If the Yankees won, they'd be the American League East champions.

With one out and Hideki Matsui on base, Bernie Williams stepped into the batter's box to face Aaron Fultz. On a 1–0 pitch, Williams hit a walk-off, pennant-winning home run.

The Yankees won their seventh straight AL East Division title.

Final score: Yankees 6, Twins 4.

OCTOBER

Of those players who have hit a minimum of 20 home runs in a single season, *only* Joe DiMaggio has seven seasons—including five in a row, 1937 to 1941—in which he had more home runs than strikeouts. This record has stood since 1948.

SEASON	HOME RUNS	STRIKEOUTS
1937	46	37
1938	32	21
1939	30	20
1940	31	30
1941	30	13
1946	25	24
1948	39	30

Had it not been for his less-than-stellar final season (12 home runs, 36 strikeouts, and a .263 batting average), DiMaggio would have had more career home runs than strikeouts. Including his stats for 1951, DiMaggio had 361 home runs and 369 strikeouts. Subtract 1951 (when the Yankees begged him to play and paid him $90,000), and he'd have had 349 home runs and 333 strikeouts.

October 1, 1921

Babe Ruth Surrenders His Final Home Run

Scene: The Polo Grounds, New York City
Attendance: 28,000

With one out in the top of the eighth inning of Game Two of a doubleheader, center fielder Frank Welch of the Philadelphia Athletics hit a home run off New York Yankees pitcher Babe Ruth.

This was the 10th and final home run given up by Babe Ruth in 163 games on the mound.

Final score: Yankees 7, A's 6.

October 1, 1932

"The Called Shot"

Scene: Wrigley Field, Chicago
Attendance: 49,986

Babe Ruth hit 714 regular-season home runs in his career, but none of those had names. The one he hit in Game Three of the 1932 World Series did. It is known as "The Called Shot."[78]

This is the version of what happened that I like the best: Infielder Mark Koenig had been a teammate of Ruth's on the Yankees from 1925 to 1930. After a brief stop with the Detroit Tigers, Koenig was obtained by the Chicago Cubs in August 1932, in time to play 33 regular-season games before the World Series. But Ruth didn't like the way Koenig was being treated by the Cubs.

---

78.   Whether it was truly a called shot is still debated. The grainy film, said to be of the incident, is informative but not dispositive.

The Yankees won the first two games of the Series at Yankee Stadium. As Ruth stepped into the batter's box in the top of the fifth inning in Game Three of the Series to face Charlie Root, Cubs bench jockeys were riding Ruth. He remonstrated with them and perhaps gesticulated toward the Cubs bench about Koenig.

After strike one, Ruth held up a finger indicating, "That's just one strike." After two balls, he took another strike, and held up two fingers.

It might have looked like he was pointing to the left-center-field stands. On Root's next pitch, a changeup, Ruth homered—right where he had "pointed" over center fielder Johnny Moore's head. There has never been anything like it in baseball.

Eleven future Hall of Famers appeared in the game: umpire Bill Klem, Ruth, Lou Gehrig, Bill Dickey, Tony Lazzeri, Earle Combs, Joe Sewell, Herb Pennock, Hazen "Kiki" Cuyler, and Gabby Hartnett—"Old Tomato Face."[79] The Yankees manager was Joe McCarthy.

Final score: New York 7, Chicago 5.

October 1, 1961

Roger Maris Hits His 61st Home Run of the 1961 Season

Scene: Yankee Stadium, New York City
Attendance: 23,154

Roger Maris (born Maras) was born in Hibbing, Minnesota. He moved to Fargo, North Dakota, and considered it his

---

79. They don't have nicknames like *that* anymore.

Roger Maris

adopted hometown. He was only twenty-two when he broke in with the Cleveland Indians in 1957.

Maris blossomed in New York, leading the American League with 112 RBIs in 1960. Mickey Mantle, his teammate and housemate, had "only" 94. Mantle—although not a native New Yorker, never played for any other team—remained the fans' favorite, while Maris had played for Cleveland and the Kansas City Athletics before coming to New York.

But 1961 turned into a historic year for baseball and for Maris. With the addition of two new teams in the American League—the Los Angeles Angels and the second Washington Senators—the season was expanded from 154 games to 162. Maris and Mantle battled for the home run lead all season until Mantle was felled by an injury—an injection-site wound that did not heal properly. Mantle had to settle for 54 round-trippers.

Maris went on to hit his record-breaking 61st home run off Tracy Stallard of the Boston Red Sox in the bottom of the fourth inning on October 1, 1961—the 162nd and last game of the season—breaking Babe Ruth's single season record of 60 that had stood since September 30, 1927. A fan named Sal Durante caught the blast.

Final Score: The pennant-winning Yankees 1, Red Sox 0.

Maris's record stood for 37 years until it was broken by Mark McGwire's 62nd home run on September 8, 1998.

October 2, 1947

Yogi Berra Hits the First Pinch-Hit Home Run in World Series History

Scene: Ebbets Field, New York City
Attendance: 33,098

With one out in the top of the seventh inning of Game Three of the 1947 World Series, the Yankees were down 9–7 to their crosstown rivals, the Brooklyn Dodgers. Yankees catcher Yogi Berra—a veteran of the Normandy

Yogi Berra

invasion[80]—pinch-hit for Sherm Lollar. Facing Ralph Branca, Berra homered to right-center field—the first pinch-hit home run in the World Series.

Final score: Brooklyn 9, Yankees 8.

October 2, 1978

The Bucky Dent Home Run

Scene: Fenway Park, Boston
Attendance: 32,925

Nineteen seventy-eight was a very exciting season, particularly in the American League East. The Boston Red Sox and the New York Yankees battled it out all season. On July 19, the Red Sox held a seemingly insurmountable 14-game lead over the Bronx Bombers. But the Yankees kept closing the gap.

Bucky Dent

On October 1, after the 162-game season, both teams had identical 99-63 records—thanks in part to a four-game Yankees sweep of the Red Sox in Boston September 7–10,[81] in which New York outscored Boston 42–9.

Following American League rules, after a coin flip to determine where the game would be played,[82] the AL East

---

80. Berra said that the D-Day invasion was noisy—"like Opening Day."
81. Dubbed "The Boston Massacre."
82. Yankee owner George Steinbrenner berated General Manager Al Rosen for *losing the coin flip!*

title would be decided in a one-game playoff—the first in the American League since 1948—at historic Fenway Park, which opened in 1912.[83]

The Red Sox had lost a dramatic 1975 World Series 4–3 to the Cincinnati Reds. The Yankees had lost the 1976 Series to the Reds but won the 1977 Series by beating the Los Angeles Dodgers.

The Yankees had three managers in 1978: Billy Martin (94 games), Dick Howser (1 game), and Hall of Famer Bob Lemon (68 games). The Boston Red Sox manager was Don Zimmer.[84]

At the end of six innings, the Yankees had only two hits, and the Red Sox were ahead 2–0. In the top of the 7th, twenty-six-year-old Yankee shortstop Russell Earl "Bucky" Dent[85] came to the plate with two outs. Chris Chambliss and Roy White were on base. The pitcher was Mike Torrez, who later pitched for the Yankees.[86] Dent had hit only four home runs all season long at that point.[87]

With the count 1–0, Dent cracked his bat on a foul ball off his right ankle and borrowed a bat from center fielder Mickey Rivers. On the next pitch, Dent hit a home run for the ages—over the Green Monster in left field to give the Yankees a 3–2 lead. New York scored again in the inning to go ahead 4–2.

When Carl Yastrzemski popped out to third baseman Graig Nettles in the bottom of the ninth, the Yankees had

---

83. This game, number 163, was not counted as a postseason contest: The usual 162-game season was now a 163-game season, and statistics accumulated in this game were included as part of the regular season.
84. Zimmer was the last Brooklyn Dodger still in uniform, unless you count Cal Abrams, who was *buried* in his Dodger uniform.
85. Like Jim Palmer, Aaron Judge, and Rob Refsnyder, Dent is an adoptee. Dent's birth name is Russell Earl O'Dey.
86. At 6'5", Torrez was eight inches taller than Dent, listed at 5'9"
87. To go with his .243 batting average and 40 RBIs.

won the game 5–4 and the AL East title. They went on to beat the Kansas City Royals 3–1 for the American League title (then a best-of-five series), then beat the Los Angeles Dodgers 4–2 to win the World Series.

Dent's home run became immortal in Yankees lore and infamous in Red Sox lore. But it did earn Dent, a future Yankee manager, a new, unprintable nickname throughout New England.

Final score: New York 5, Boston 4.

October 3, 1926

Tommy Thevenow Hits an Inside-the-Park Home Run in the World Series

Scene: Yankee Stadium, New York City
Attendance: 63,600

World Series, Game Two—in the top of the ninth inning, twenty-three-year-old St. Louis Cardinals shortstop Tommy Thevenow hit an inside-the-park home run to right field off New York Yankees pitcher "Sad" Sam Jones.

Final score: Cardinals 6, Yankees 2.

October 3, 1965

Tony Kubek Homers in His Final At-Bat

Scene: Fenway Park, Boston
Attendance: 5,933

It was the last day of the 1965 season. Also, thanks to three crushed vertebrae as a child, it would be the final game for twenty-nine-year-old Tony Kubek, the Yankees shortstop for nine seasons.

Kubek was 2-for-3 when he came to bat in the top of the ninth inning to face 6'6" Boston Red Sox pitcher Dick Radatz, nicknamed "The Monster," with Roger Repoz on base. Kubek homered—his memorable final at-bat. Final score: Yankees 11, Red Sox 5.

This was Yankees pitcher Whitey Ford's 232nd win—breaking Red Ruffing's record of 231 wins, set in 1946, for most wins by a Yankees pitcher. Ford retired in 1967 with 236 wins—after 50 years, still the Yankees record.

Kubek went on to an outstanding broadcasting career and earned the Ford C. Frick Award for broadcasting at the Baseball Hall of Fame in 2009.

October 3, 1999

Randy Winn Hits an Inside-the-Park Grand Slam

Scene: Tropicana Field, St. Petersburg, Florida
Attendance: 31,292

In the bottom of the first inning, Tampa Bay Devil Rays center fielder Randy Winn was called out on strikes. He walked in the third inning but was erased on a double play. Things improved for Winn in the fourth inning, though.

With the score tied at two, two outs, and the bases loaded with José Guillén, Terrell Lowery, and David Lamb, Winn faced New York Yankees starter Jeff Juden. Winn's blast hit the center-field wall and eluded center fielder Chad Curtis. Winn scored—an inside-the-park grand slam.

That day, the final game of the season, the Yankees were managed by right fielder Paul O'Neill.

Final score: Tampa Bay 6, Yankees 2.

October 4, 2009

Alex Rodriguez Hits the Yankees Record
243rd and 244th Home Runs

Scene: Tropicana Field, Saint Petersburg, Florida
Attendance: 28,699

On the last day of the 2009 season, New York Yankees third baseman Alex Rodriguez smashed 2 homers in the sixth inning. Johnny Damon and Mark Teixeira were on base for the 1st, hit off Tampa Bay Rays pitcher Wade Davis. For the 2nd, José Molina, Brett Gardner, and Juan Miranda were on base. The pitcher was Andy Sonnanstine.

In the process, Rodriguez became one of the rare players to homer in his first at-bat of the season—on May 2—and last at-bat of the season.

These were the Yankees' 243rd and 244th home runs of the season—a team record.

Final score: Yankees 10, Rays 2.

October 5, 1912

Hal Chase Hits the Final Homer at Hilltop Park

Scene: Hilltop Park, New York City
Attendance: 2,000—14,000 empty seats

In the bottom of the eighth inning, New York Highlanders (Yankees) first baseman Harold Homer "Hal" Chase hits a home run off Washington Senators pitcher Clark Griffith, a future Hall of Famer, with two men on base. Chase's home run was the last one at Hilltop Park.

This was the Highlanders' final game of the season and their last game at Hilltop Park, built at 168th Street and Broadway on what was said to be the highest point in Manhattan.

The next year, the Highlanders played their home games at the Polo Grounds, where they were tenants of the New York Giants.

Final score: New York 8, Washington 6.

October 5, 1926

Jesse Haines Hits the First World Series Home Run West of the Mississippi

Scene: Sportsman's Park, St. Louis
Attendance: 37,708

With Tommy Thevenow on base in the bottom of the fourth inning of Game Three of the World Series, St. Louis Cardinals pitcher Jesse Haines[88] homered off Yankees pitcher Walter "Dutch" Ruether.

Final score: Cardinals 4, Yankees 0 in a game that took only one hour and 41 minutes, with a 30-minute rain delay. Haines got the win.

This was the first World Series home run west of the Mississippi. Sportsman's Park, home to both the St. Louis Cardinals and the Browns, was just west of the river.

Eleven future Hall of Famers participated in this game: umpires Bill Klem and Hank O'Day, Haines, Ruth, Lou Gehrig, Tony Lazzeri, Billy Southworth,[89] "Sunny" Jim Bottomley, Earle Combs, Chick Hafey, and Rogers Hornsby.

---

88. Haines is the only major leaguer from Clayton, Ohio.
89. Southworth is the only native of Harvard, Nebraska, to play major-league baseball.

The first Yankee to homer west of the Mississippi was Babe Ruth, who homered in Game Four of the 1926 Series on October 6. In fact, Ruth homered three times in that game.

October 5, 1949

Tommy Henrich Hits a Walk-Off Home Run in Game One of the World Series

Scene: Yankee Stadium, New York City
Attendance: 66,224

Game One of the 1949 World Series was a pitcher's duel between Don Newcombe of the Brooklyn Dodgers and Allie Reynolds of the New York Yankees, both of whom pitched complete games.

There was still no score in the bottom of the ninth inning when Yankees first baseman Tommy Henrich—"Old Reliable"—smacked a 2–0 slider for a walk-off home run.

Eight future Hall of Famers appeared in this game: umpire Cal Hubbard,[90] Jackie Robinson, Pee Wee Reese, Duke Snider, Roy Campanella, Phil Rizzuto, Yogi Berra, and Joe DiMaggio.

Henrich's home run was the first to decide a World Series game by a 1–0 score since Casey Stengel's home run for the New York Giants in Game Three of the 1923 World Series, the first at Yankee Stadium. Stengel was the Yankees manager in 1949.

Final score: Yankees 1, Dodgers 0.

---

90. Hubbard is the only man elected to the Pro Football Hall of Fame, the College Football Hall of Fame, and the Baseball Hall of Fame.

October 5, 1957

Rookie Tony Kubek Hits Two Home Runs in One World Series Game in His Hometown

Scene: County Stadium, Milwaukee
Attendance: 45,804

Game Three of the World Series marked the first World Series game ever in Milwaukee.

In the top of the first inning, twenty-one-year-old New York Yankees rookie shortstop Tony Kubek—a Milwaukee native—homered off Bob Buhl of the Milwaukee Braves.

In the Yankees' five-run seventh inning, Kubek homered again, this time off Bob Trowbridge with Don Larsen and Hank Bauer on base.

Kubek was only the second rookie to smash two round-trippers in a World Series game. The first was another Yankee, Charlie "King Kong" Keller, on October 8, 1939, in Game Three. Kubek was the 1957 American League Rookie of the Year.

Eight future Hall of Famers were on the field for this game: umpires Nestor Chylak and Jocko Conlan, Yankees manager Casey Stengel, Mickey Mantle, Yogi Berra, Red Schoendienst, Hank Aaron, and Eddie Mathews.

Final score: Yankees 12, Braves 3.

October 6, 1926

Babe Ruth Hits Three Home Runs in One World Series Game

Scene: Sportsman's Park, St. Louis
Attendance: 38,825

With two outs in the top of the first inning of Game Four of the World Series, Babe Ruth of the Yankees homered off Charles "Flint" Rhem[91] of the St. Louis Cardinals. Ruth homered again off Rhem in the third.

In the sixth inning with one out and Earle Combs on base, Ruth hit his 3rd home run of the game, this one off Hi Bell.

Ruth was the first man to hit 3 home runs in a World Series game.[92]

Eleven future Hall of Famers participated in this game: umpire Bill Klem, Yankees manager Miller Huggins, Ruth, Combs, Lou Gehrig, Tony Lazzeri, Waite Hoyt, Billy Southworth, Rogers Hornsby, "Sunny" Jim Bottomley, and Charles "Chick" Hafey.

Final score: Yankees 10, Cardinals 5.

October 6, 1957

A Walk-Off Home Run in the World Series

Scene: County Stadium, Milwaukee
Attendance: 45,804

The Yankees were up 5–4 going into the bottom of the 10th inning of Game Four of the World Series. With Milwaukee Braves shortstop Johnny Logan on base and one out, third baseman Eddie Mathews stepped up to face New York City native Bob Grim, the fifth Yankees pitcher. Using one of Joe Adcock's 33-ounce knobless bats, Mathews hit a fastball for a walk-off 2-run home run.

---

91. Rhem is the only major league player from Rhems, South Carolina.
92. Ruth is also the first player to hit 3 home runs in a World Series game *twice*. See entry for October 9,1928.

Ten future Hall of Famers were on the field for this game: umpires Jocko Conlan and Nestor Chylak, Yankees manager Casey Stengel, Mathews, Mickey Mantle, Enos Slaughter, Yogi Berra, Red Schoendienst, Hank Aaron, and Warren Spahn.

Final score: Braves 7, Yankees 5.

October 6, 1995

Bernie Williams: First Man to Switch-Hit Home Runs in a Post-Season Game

Scene: The Kingdome, Seattle
Attendance: 57,944

With no outs and nobody on, Bernabe "Bernie" Williams of the Yankees faced Randy Johnson of the Seattle Mariners in the fourth inning of Game Three of the first American League Division Series. Williams, batting righty, homered.

In the eighth inning, with the Mariners up 7–2, Williams batted lefty to face Bill Risley and hit a solo home run— becoming the first batter to switch-hit home runs in a post-season game.

Final score: Mariners 7, Yankees 4.

October 7, 1928

Lou Gehrig Hits an Inside-the-Park Home Run in the World Series

Scene: Sportsman's Park, St. Louis
Attendance: 39,602

In Game Three of the 1928 World Series against the St. Louis Cardinals, Lou Gehrig of the Yankees homered in the second inning off Jesse Haines. When Gehrig came to bat in the fourth inning, Babe Ruth was on first base. Haines was still on the mound. Gehrig scorched a low line drive past center fielder Taylor Douthit and scored on an inside-the-park home run—becoming just the fourth player to hit 2 home runs in one World Series game.

Ten future Hall of Famers participated in this game: umpire Bill McGowan; Yankees Gehrig, Ruth, Tony Lazzeri, and Leo Durocher; and Cardinals Frankie Frisch, "Sunny" Jim Bottomley, Chick Hafey, Walter "Rabbit" Maranville, and Haines.

Final score: Yankees 7, Cardinals 3.

October 7, 1939

Charlie Keller: First Rookie to Hit Two Home Runs in One World Series Game

Scene: Crosley Field, Cincinnati
Attendance: 32,723

During Game Three of the World Series, with Frank Crosetti on base in the top of the first inning, twenty-three-year-old Yankees rookie right fielder Charlie "King Kong" Keller homered into the bleachers in right field off Eugene "Junior" Thompson of the Cincinnati Reds.

In the fifth inning, Keller homered to the right-field stands again off Thompson with Red Rolfe on base, becoming the first rookie to hit 2 home runs in one World Series game.

Eight future Hall of Famers were on the field for this game: umpire Bill McGowan, Joe DiMaggio, Joe Gordon, Bill Dickey, Ernie Lombardi, Al Simmons, Reds manager Bill McKechnie, and Yankee manager Joe McCarthy.

Final score: Yankees 7, Reds 3.

October 8, 1962

Chuck Hiller Hits the First National League Grand Slam in World Series History

Scene: Yankee Stadium, New York City
Attendance: 66,607

World Series Game Four against the San Francisco Giants was tied at 2 in the top of the seventh inning with Jim Davenport, Matty Alou, and Ernie Bowman on base for the Giants when Chuck Hiller[93] came to bat against Marshall Bridges. Hiller homered—the first National Leaguer to hit a grand slam in the World Series.

Seven future Hall of Famers appeared in this game: umpire Al Barlick, Whitey Ford, Yogi Berra, Mickey Mantle, Juan Marichal, Orlando Cepeda, and Willie Mays.

Final score: Giants 7, Yankees 3.

October 9, 1921

Babe Ruth Hits the First Yankees Home Run in the World Series

Scene: The Polo Grounds, New York City
Attendance: 36,372

World Series Game Four took place between the Yankees and the New York Giants at the stadium they shared, the Polo Grounds. In the bottom of the ninth inning, Babe Ruth of the Yankees batted against Phil Douglas.[94] Ruth homered—the first World Series home run by a Yankee.

Final score: Giants 4, Yankees 2.

---

93. Hiller is the only major leaguer from Johnsburg, Illinois.
94. Douglas is the only native of Cedartown, Georgia, to play in the major leagues.

October 9, 1928

Babe Ruth Becomes the First Man to Hit Three Home Runs in a World Series Game Twice

Scene: Sportsman's Park, St. Louis
Attendance: 37,331

Babe Ruth of the Yankees homered to lead off the top of the fourth inning of Game Four of the 1928 World Series—a solo shot off Bill Sherdel of the St. Louis Cardinals.

With one out in the seventh inning, Ruth homered again, also off Sherdel.

In the eighth inning, with one out, Ruth faced Grover Cleveland Alexander[95] and hit his record 3rd home run of the game.

Ruth, who had homered three times in Game Four of the World Series on October 6, 1926, became the first player to homer three times in a World Series game on two separate occasions.

Twelve future Hall of Famers participated in this game: umpire Bill McGowan; Yankees Ruth, Lou Gehrig, Tony Lazzeri, Leo Durocher, Earle Combs,[96] and Waite Hoyt; and Cardinals Frankie Frisch, "Sunny" Jim Bottomley, Charles "Chick" Hafey, Walter "Rabbit" Maranville, and Alexander.

Three New York City natives, all of whom wound up in Cooperstown, appeared in this game: Gehrig, Hoyt, and Frisch.

Final score: Yankees 7, Cardinals 3.

---

95. From Elba, Nebraska.
96. From Pebworth, Kentucky.

October 9, 1951

A World Series Grand Slam for Gil McDougald

Scene: The Polo Grounds, New York City
Attendance: 47,530

After Game Four of the World Series, twenty-three-year old New York Yankees rookie infielder Gil McDougald promised his father that he'd try to hit a home run in the next game. McDougald came to bat in the top of the third inning of Game Five with three future Hall of Famers on base: Yogi Berra, Joe DiMaggio, and Johnny Mize. The pitcher was Larry Jansen[97] of the New York Giants.

On a chest-high fastball, McDougald uncorked a grand slam into the stands in left field—just the third in the history of the World Series. The first two were by Elmer Smith on October 10, 1920, and Tony Lazzeri on October 2, 1936.

Eight future Hall of Famers participated in this game: umpire Al Barlick, Yankees manager Casey Stengel, Phil Rizzuto, Mize, Berra, DiMaggio, Monte Irvin, and Willie Mays.

Final score: Yankees 13, Giants 1.

October 9, 1996

The "Jeffrey Maier" Home Run

Scene: Yankee Stadium, New York City
Attendance: 56,495

The Baltimore Orioles led 4–3 in the bottom of the eighth inning of Game One of the American League Championship Series with the New York Yankees.

---

97. Jansen is the only native of Verboort, Oregon, to play in the major leagues.

With one out, Yankees shortstop Derek Jeter hit an Armando Benítez pitch over the wall in right field.

Jeffrey Maier, a 12-year-old fan, leaned over the wall to try to catch the ball. But it bounced off his glove and into the stands. Home run! Baltimore manager Davey Johnson lost an argument with right-field umpire Rich Garcia and was ejected. It was a home run. Jeffrey Maier was a new Yankees hero.

The game stayed tied at 4 until Bernie Williams led off the bottom of the 11th inning with a walk-off home run off Randy Myers.

Final score: Yankees 5, Orioles 4.

October 10, 1923

Casey Stengel Wins Game One of the 1923 World Series with an Inside-the-Park Home Run in the First World Series Game Ever Played at Yankee Stadium

Scene: Yankee Stadium, New York City
Attendance: 55,307

Game One of the 1923 World Series—the first World Series game ever played at Yankee Stadium—was unusual. The Yankees had been tenants of the Giants in the Polo Grounds, until they started to outdraw the Giants. Then the Giants kicked them out, and construction began on Yankee Stadium, the "House that Ruth Built," at 161st Street and River Avenue in the Bronx, the most famous address in baseball.

The left fielders in this game were brothers: Bob Meusel for the Yankees and Emil "Irish" Meusel for the Giants.[98]

---

98. Bob and Irish Meusel faced each other in three consecutive World Series, all in New York City: 1921, 1922, and 1923.

With the score tied at 4 in the top of the ninth inning, with two outs and none on, Giants center fielder Casey Stengel hit an inside-the-park home run, the 1st World Series homer at Yankee Stadium.

Eight future Hall of Famers appeared in this game: umpires Billy Evans and Hank O'Day, Stengel, Babe Ruth, Dave "Beauty" Bancroft, and Ross Youngs,[99] plus New York City natives Frankie Frisch and Waite Hoyt.

Final score: Giants 5, Yankees 4.

October 10, 1964

Mickey Mantle Breaks Babe Ruth's World Series Home Run Record

Scene: Yankee Stadium, New York City
Attendance: 67,101

Before one of the largest crowds in baseball history, the Yankees and the St. Louis Cardinals were tied at 1 from the fifth inning on of Game Three of the World Series. Then, in the bottom of the ninth, George "Barney" Schultz came in to pitch for the Cardinals. The first batter he faced was Yankees center fielder Mickey Mantle. On Schultz's first pitch, Mantle connected for a titanic walk-off home run deep into the right field stands.

This was Mantle's 16th World Series home run, breaking a tie at 15 with Babe Ruth.

Final score: Yankees 2, Cardinals 1. The winning pitcher was Jim Bouton, who pitched a complete game.[100]

---

99. From Shiner, Texas. Thirty years old when he died in 1927, Youngs is the youngest player in the Baseball Hall of Fame.

100. Bouton, author of the seminal *Ball Four*, is a native of Newark, New Jersey. Schultz, the losing pitcher, is from Beverly, New Jersey, just 60 miles from Newark.

Mickey Mantle

October 12, 1923

Casey Stengel Hits His Second Homer of the World Series

Scene: Yankee Stadium, New York City
Attendance: 62,430[101]

With one out in the top of the seventh inning of Game Three of the World Series, facing New York Yankees pitcher "Sad" Sam Jones,[102] New York Giants center fielder Charles Dillon "Casey" Stengel hit his 2nd home run of the Series. His 1st was in Game One on October 10.

---

101. This was the largest crowd in baseball history up to this time.
102. There were two big league pitchers named Sam Jones. Both pitched no-hitters.

Ten future Hall of Famers appeared in this game: umpires Hank O'Day and Billy Evans, Yankees manager Miller Huggins, Giants manager John McGraw, plus Stengel, Dave "Beauty" Bancroft, Frankie Frisch—"The Fordham Flash," Ross Youngs, George "High Pockets" Kelly, and Babe Ruth.

Emil "Irish" Meusel was playing left field for the Giants. His younger brother Bob was the Yankees' left fielder. In the first inning, Bob flied out to Irish. In the second, Irish flied out to Bob.

Final score: Giants 1, Yankees 0.

October 13, 1923

Ross Youngs Hits an Inside-the-Park Home Run in the World Series

Scene: The Polo Grounds, New York City
Attendance: 46,302

In the ninth inning of Game Four of the 1923 World Series, 26-year-old New York Giants right fielder Ross (born Royce) Youngs hit a ball off Yankees pitcher Herb Pennock to right field. Youngs circled the bases for an inside-the-park home run.

Nine future Hall of Famers appeared in this game: umpires Hank O'Day and Billy Evans, Yankees Babe Ruth and Herb Pennock, and Giants Youngs, Dave Bancroft, Frankie Frisch, Casey Stengel, and George "High Pockets" Kelly.

Final score: Yankees 8, Giants 4.

October 13, 1960

Bill Mazeroski Hits the Only Seventh-Game Walk-Off Home Run in World Series History

Scene: Forbes Field, Pittsburgh
Attendance: 36,683

The 1960 World Series was unusual for many reasons. The New York Yankees, the *losing* team, outscored the winning Pittsburgh Pirates 55 to 27. The MVP of the series, second baseman Bobby Richardson, played on the losing team.

But perhaps most unusual of all, the game ended on a walk-off home run in the bottom of the ninth inning—through 2017, the only Game Seven walk-off home run in World Series history.

The score was tied at 9 as the Yankees, winners of 97 regular-season games, faced the Pirates, who won 95 during the regular season. The first batter for Pittsburgh was Bill Mazeroski, the Pirates' light-hitting (.260 career batting average) second baseman. Maz had hit eleven (11) home runs during the regular season and only 138 during his 17-year (1956–1972) career, all with the Pirates. Maz hit Ralph Terry's[103] pitch over Yankees left-fielder Yogi Berra's head and into the left-field stands and history.

Final score: Pirates 10, Yankees 9.[104] Mickey Mantle cried in the clubhouse after this game.

---

103. From Big Cabin, Oklahoma.
104. After Mazeroski's 2001 induction into the Baseball Hall of Fame, primarily on the basis of this single home run, a fan got a license plate reading MAZISIN.

October 14, 1923

Joe Dugan Hits an Inside-the-Park Home Run in the World Series

Scene: Yankee Stadium, New York City
Attendance: 62,817[105]

In the bottom of the second inning of Game Five of the 1923 World Series, with one out and Bullet Joe Bush and Whitey Witt on base, "Jumping" Joe Dugan of the Yankees hit a ball to shallow center field off New York Giants pitcher Jack Bentley. Casey Stengel and Ross Youngs ran for it, but the ball bounced off Stengel's glove and rolled to the wall while Dugan circled the bases for an inside-the-park home run.

Eight future Hall of Famers were in this game—umpires Billy Evans and Hank O'Day, plus Babe Ruth for the Yankees,[106] and Stengel, Youngs, Dave "Beauty" Bancroft, Bronx native Frankie Frisch—"The Fordham Flash," and George "High Pockets" Kelly for the Giants.

Final score: Yankees 8, Giants 1.

October 14, 1976

Chris Chambliss's Unforgettable Home Run

Scene: Yankee Stadium, New York City
Attendance: 56,821

Nineteen seventy-one American League Rookie of the Year Chris Chambliss was a first baseman for the Cleveland

---

105. This was the largest crowd to watch a baseball game up to this time. Another 40,000 were turned away. The gate was $201,459, a record at the time.

106. The Yankees used only the nine players who started the game: no pitching changes, no pinch-hitters, and no pinch-runners.

Indians, New York Yankees, and Atlanta Braves from 1971 to 1988.

He hit 185 career home runs and played on World Championship Yankees teams in 1977 and 1978.

But he will always be remembered for the walk-off home run he hit into the right-center-field stands—and into history—in the bottom of the ninth inning in the deciding

Chris Chambliss

Game Five of the 1976 American League Championship Series against the Kansas City Royals, champions of the American League West. With the game tied at 6, Chambliss's smash off Mark Littell put the Yankees into their first World Series since 1962.

Chambliss was mobbed by Yankees fans who poured onto the field as he rounded first base. When he finally made it to the Yankees clubhouse 10 minutes later, he was told that he had not stepped on home plate. He went back out on the field and definitively stepped on the plate. Royals shortstop Freddie Patek cried on the Royals' bench.

Final score: Yankees 7, Royals 6.

October 15, 1964

Mickey Mantle Hits His Record 18th World Series Home Run

Scene: Busch Stadium, St. Louis
Attendance: 30,346

Mickey Mantle

Mickey Mantle, the only native of Spavinaw, Oklahoma, to play in the majors, appeared in 65 World Series games in 12 seasons.

Game Seven of the 1964 World Series was the 65th World Series game in which Mantle had played,[107] and the last one of his 18-year career—all with the New York Yankees.

In the top the sixth inning, with Bobby Richardson and Roger Maris on base with no outs, Mantle faced St. Louis Cardinals pitcher Bob Gibson—who, like Mantle, was a future Hall of Famer. Mantle blasted a 3-run home run—his 3rd home run of the 1964 Series and the record 18th World Series round-tripper of his career.

Final score: Cardinals 7, Yankees 5.

---

107. Yogi Berra still holds the record: 75.

October 16, 2003

Aaron Boone's 11th-Inning Walk-Off Home Run Blasts the Yankees into the World Series

Scene: Yankee Stadium, New York City
Attendance: 56,279

Few things in sports are as exciting as a Game Seven in a baseball playoff series. So it was when the Boston Red Sox and the New York Yankees met for the deciding Game Seven of the American League Championship Series on October 16, 2003.

In the bottom of the 11th inning, the game—which had taken nearly four hours, typical for a game between these long-time rivals—was tied at 5. The two teams had used 33 players, including 10 pitchers. Knuckleballer Tim Wakefield was on the mound for Boston. The leadoff hitter for New York was Aaron Boone, who had entered the game as a pinch-runner in the eighth inning. Boone had gone 5 for 31 in the playoffs.

Boone had baseball in his DNA, though: his grandfather Ray, father Bob, and brother Bret[108] were all big-leaguers.

In his final Yankees regular season at-bat,[109] Boone hit Wakefield's first pitch into the left-field bleachers—a game- and pennant-winning walk-off home run, and one of the most glorious in Yankees history.

Final score: Yankees 6, Red Sox 5.

---

108. Bret Boone was broadcasting this game for FOX Sports.
109. On March 1, 2004, Boone was released. Thanks!

October 18, 1977

Reggie Jackson Hits Three Home Runs in a World Series Game

Scene: Yankee Stadium, New York City
Attendance: 56,407

The Yankees led the 1977 World Series 3 games to 2 when they played the Los Angeles Dodgers in Game Six. Joltin' Joe DiMaggio—the "Yankee Clipper"—threw out the ceremonial first pitch. President Jimmy Carter's mother Lillian, a Dodgers fan, was at the game.

Reggie Jackson

In the bottom of the fourth inning, Reginald Martinez "Reggie" Jackson—"Mr. October"—came to bat against Burt Hooton. With Thurman Munson on base, Jackson blasted Hooton's first pitch into the right-field stands.

Jackson batted again with two outs in the fifth inning, this time with Willie Randolph on base. True to his name, Mr. October blasted the first pitch from Elias Sosa, a drive into the right-field seats this time.

Jackson led off the eighth inning with a home run on the first pitch from Charlie Hough[110]—a 450-foot blast to the center-field bleachers—for the last of 3 home runs,[111] each

---

110. Hough finished his career with a record of 216 wins and 216 losses.
111. In the top of the eighth inning of Game Five played on October 16 at Dodger Stadium, Jackson hit a home run that hit the foul pole in right field. The Dodgers won that Game One 10–4. Thus, Jackson hit home runs on four consecutive swings of the bat in the World Series.

on the first pitch, off three pitchers in one game of the World Series.

Final score: Yankees 8, Dodgers 4. The Yankees were World Champions.

Jackson hit a record 5 homers in the 1977 World Series, set the record with 25 total bases, scored a record 10 runs, and tied Babe Ruth for most total bases in a game—12.

October 19, 1976

First Desigated Hitter to Homer in the World Series

Scene: Yankee Stadium, New York City
Attendance: 56,667

Dan Driessen,[112] usually a utility player for the Cincinnati Reds, had an unfamiliar role in Game Three of the 1976 World Series when he led off the top of the fourth inning, facing Dock Ellis[113] at Yankee Stadium; Driessen hit the 1st World Series home run by a designated hitter.

Final score: Reds 6, Yankees 2.

October 19, 1976

Jim Mason Hits the First Home Run for the Yankees in a World Series Night Game

Scene: Yankee Stadium, New York City
Attendance: 56,667

---

112. A native of Hilton Head Island, South Carolina.
113. True first name: "Dock."

In the bottom of the seventh inning of World Series Game Three, Yankees shortstop Jim Mason homered off Cincinnati Reds pitcher Pat Zachry. Mason's blast was the 1st home run by a Yankee in a World Series night game at Yankee Stadium. Final score: Reds 6, Yankees 2.

October 20, 1931
Mickey Mantle Is Born

Mickey Mantle, who hit 536 career home runs—all for the New York Yankees—was born in Spavinaw, Oklahoma.

October 20, 1996
Andruw Jones Hits Two Home Runs in His First World Series Game

Scene: Yankee Stadium, New York City
Attendance: 56,365

After winning the World Series in 1995, the Atlanta Braves faced the New York Yankees in the 1996 Fall Classic.

In the top of the second inning of Game One, Javy López was on base when nineteen-year-old Braves left fielder Andruw Jones[114] homered off Andy Pettitte of the New York Yankees— the youngest man ever to hit a World Series home run.

---

114. Jones is a native of Willemstad, Curaçao. He was knighted by Queen Beatrix of the Netherlands in 2011. Jones hit 51 round-trippers in 2005 and retired in 2012 with 434 career home runs after a 17-year career. Neither Sir Tim Keefe, Sir Hugh Duffy, nor Duff Cooley (a.k.a. Sir Richard) was ever officially knighted.

Jones homered again in the third inning with Fred McGriff and Lopez aboard, this time off Brian Boehringer—the first player to hit 2 home runs in his first two World Series at-bats since Gene Tenace of the Oakland Athletics on October 14, 1972.

Final score: Braves 12, Yankees 1.

October 23, 1996

Jim Leyritz Hits a 3-Run Home Run in Game Four of the 1996 World Series

Scene: Atlanta-Fulton County Stadium
Attendance: 51,881

In the top of the sixth inning of Game Four of the 1996 World Series, Paul O'Neill batted for catcher (and future Yankees manager) Joe Girardi. O'Neill struck out.

In the top of the eighth inning, with the Atlanta Braves leading the game 6–3 and the Series 2 games to 1, catcher Jim Leyritz—who was never drafted—was batting. Mark Wohlers was on the

Jim Leyritz

mound for the Braves. Charlie Hayes and Mariano Duncan were on base.

Leyritz hit a 3-run home run that tied the game and electrified the Yankees.

Final score: Yankees 8, Braves 6 in 10 innings.

October 25, 2000

Derek Jeter Leads Off Game Four of the 2000 World Series with a Home Run

Scene: Shea Stadium, New York City
Attendance: 55,290

Twenty-six-year-old Yankees shortstop Derek Jeter led off the top of the first inning of Game Four of the 2000 Subway World Series with a home run off Bobby J. Jones of the New York Mets.[115]

Final score: Yankees 3, Mets 2.

October 27, 1999

Jim Leyritz Hits the Last Home Run of the Twentieth Century

Scene: Yankee Stadium, New York City
Attendance: 56,752

With the bases empty and two outs in the bottom of the eighth inning of Game Four of the 1999 World Series—the final game of the twentieth century—New York Yankee Jim Leyritz pinch-hit for Darryl Strawberry. Leyritz homered on a pitch from Terry Mulholland of the Atlanta Braves—the final home run of the twentieth century.

Final score: Yankees 4, Braves 1.

---

115. Not to be confused with Bobby M. Jones, who also pitched for the Mets in 2000.

October 28, 2001

Matt Williams Hits a World Series Home Run for His Third Team

Scene: Bank One Ballpark, Phoenix
Attendance: 49,646

During Game Two of the World Series, Reggie Sanders and Danny Bautista were on base with two outs in the bottom of the seventh inning when Arizona Diamondbacks third baseman Matt Williams[116] homered off New York Yankees starter Andy Pettitte.

Williams, who had homered for the Cleveland Indians in the 1997 Series and the San Francisco Giants in the 1989 fall classic, became the first player to homer for three different teams in the World Series.

Final score: Arizona 4, New York 0.

October 28, 2009

Chase Utley Homers in the World Series

Scene: Yankee Stadium II, New York City
Attendance: 50,207

With two outs in the top of the third inning of Game One of the World Series, thirty-year-old Philadelphia Phillies second baseman Chase Utley homered against Yankee C. C. Sabathia. With one out in the sixth inning, Utley homered off Sabathia again.

---

116. Williams is the only major leaguer born in Bishop, California.

Utley was the first lefty batter to homer twice in a World Series game off a left-handed pitcher in 81 seasons. The last batter to accomplish this unusual feat was Babe Ruth of the Yankees in Game Four of the 1928 World Series when he hit 2 solo blasts off St. Louis Cardinal Bill Sherdel.[117] In that game, Ruth hit a historic 3rd homer too, this one off Grover Cleveland Alexander.

Final score: Phillies 6, Yankees 1.

October 31, 2009

Alex Rodriguez Hits a ~~Double~~ Home Run

Scene: Citizens Bank Ballpark, Philadelphia
Attendance: 46,061

In the top of the fourth inning of Game Three of the World Series, with Mark Teixeira on base, Yankees third baseman Alex Rodriguez blasted a pitch from Cole Hamels of the Philadelphia Phillies toward the right-field foul pole. The blast hit a TV camera and bounced back onto the field. Right-field umpire Jeff Nelson called the ball in play, and it was ruled a double.

But Yankees manager Joe Girardi disagreed, so Gerry Davis, the left-field umpire and crew chief, called for a video review, after which the call was overturned. The ball was ruled a 2-run home run—the first video replay in postseason play.

Final score: Yankees 8, Phillies 5.

---

117. Sherdel is one of only three big-leaguers born in McSherrystown, Pennsylvania.

NOVEMBER

DID YOU KNOW?

When he smashed his 52nd and final home run of the season on September 30, 2017—the new rookie record—Aaron Judge of the Yankees broke a different record, which had stood since Babe Ruth set it more than half a century before: most home runs at home in a single season by a Yankee. Ruth hit 32 home runs at home at the Polo Grounds in 1921. Judge's 52nd home run of 2017 was his 33rd at Yankee Stadium II.

November 1, 2001

Derek Jeter Hits the First Home Run in November

Scene: Yankee Stadium, New York City
Attendance: 55,863[118]

In the aftermath of the September 11, 2001, terrorist attacks on the World Trade Center in New York City, the Pentagon, and Shanksville, Pennsylvania, Major League Baseball suspended all games for six days. The World Series didn't start until October 27, the latest start ever.

Game Four—a night game between the Arizona Diamondbacks and the New York Yankees—began on Halloween, October 31. By the time Derek Jeter came to bat in the bottom of the 10th inning, with the game tied at three, the clock had moved past midnight. The message board flashed: ATTENTION FANS: WELCOME TO NOVEMBER BASEBALL.

After fouling off three pitches, with two outs and a 3–2 count, the Yankees shortstop ended the game with a home run off Byung-Hyun Kim that landed in the first row of the right-field seats. Jeter circled the bases with his right fist in the air. He had just hit the first major-league home run in November. After seven years in the majors, with 99 regular season home runs and 8 (now 9) postseason blasts, it was also Jeter's first walk-off home run.

Final score: Yankees 4, Diamondbacks 3.

November 1, 2001

First Baseball Game to Start in November

Scene: Yankee Stadium, New York City
Attendance: 56,018

---

118. Including me.

The first major-league game to start in the month of November was Game Five of this World Series.

Two Arizona Diamondbacks homered in the top of the fifth inning. Steve Finley connected off New York Yankees pitcher Mike Mussina, and later in the inning, Rod Barajas hit a solo homer off Mussina.

In the bottom of the ninth inning, Yankees third baseman Scott Brosius hit a 2-run blast off pitcher Byung-Hyun Kim.

Final score: Yankees 3, Diamondbacks 2 in 12 innings.

November 2, 2009

Chase Utley Hits His Fifth Home Run of the World Series

Scene: Citizens Bank Park, Philadelphia
Attendance: 46,178

In Game One of the 2009 World Series, thirty-year-old Philadelphia Phillies second baseman Chase Utley connected for 2 home runs against the Yankees' C. C. Sabathia.

He hit a 3rd in Game Four on November 1, a seventh-inning blast, also off Sabathia.

In the top of the first inning of Game Five, with Jimmy Rollins and Shane Victorino on base, Utley hit a home run off A. J. Burnett.

Utley homered again in the seventh inning off Phil Coke.

Utley is the second player, after Willie Mays Aikens in 1980, to have two multi–home run games in one World Series.

Final score: Phillies 8, Yankees 6 in three hours, 26 minutes.

November 4, 2001

Alfonso Soriano Hits the Latest Home Run Ever

Scene: Bank One Ballpark, Phoenix
Attendance: 49,589

Because of the attacks of September 11, 2001, no Major League Baseball games were played between September 12 and September 16.

Yankees second baseman Alfonso Soriano led off the eighth inning of Game Seven of the World Series with a home run off Anchorage, Alaska, native Curt Schilling of the Arizona Diamondbacks—the latest home run ever, at that point. Ryan Howard and Hideki Matsui subsequently homered on November 4 in 2009, World Series Game Six.

Final score: Diamondbacks 3, Yankees 2.

November 13, 1998

The Ball Babe Ruth Hit for His First Home Run at Yankee Stadium Sells at Auction for $126,500

In an auction held in New York City, the winning bid of $126,500 was made by phone for the ball that Babe Ruth hit on April 18, 1923—Opening Day at Yankee Stadium.

November 29, 1976

Reggie Jackson Signs a $3.5 Million Contract

The Yankees signed free agent Reggie Jackson to a five-year contract for $3.5 million—an enormous sum at the time.

During his five years (1977–1981) with the Yankees, Jackson hit 144 regular-season home runs (plus 12 postseason home runs) and helped the team win two world championships.

DECEMBER

December 11, 1959

Roger Maris Is Traded from the Kansas City Athletics to the New York Yankees

Twenty-five-year-old Roger Maris, Kent Hadley, and Joe DeMaestri were traded to the New York Yankees by the Kansas City Athletics for Norm Siebern, Marv Throneberry, Hank Bauer, and Don Larsen.

December 14, 1985

Roger Maris Dies

Roger Maris, who hit 61 home runs for the Yankees in 1961, died in Houston at age 51.

ABOUT THE AUTHOR

Douglas B. Lyons has *not* been a baseball fan all his life. He was born in New York City, the youngest of four brothers. His oldest brother George was a fan of the St. Louis Cardinals for more than 60 years.[119] Likewise, his brother Jeffrey has been a fan of the Boston Red Sox for more than 60 years.

Douglas Lyons's first baseball glove was a Bob Feller model, given to him by Bob Feller himself, a friend of his parents. He did not become a baseball fan until 1972, when, at age 25, he read Jim Bouton's seminal book, *Ball Four*. Since then, he has become an avid fan. A member of the Society for American Baseball Research (SABR), he has spoken at the Smithsonian, the National Baseball Hall of Fame in Cooperstown, Fenway Park in Boston, and national and regional SABR conventions.

The only baseball memorabilia he collects are pins and bobble-head dolls.

In his spare time, he is a criminal lawyer in New York City. He has been married for over 41 years. He and his wife have four children and one grandchild.

---

119. George's license plate said BASEBALL. George was buried in his Cardinals shirt.

INDEX

What I learned while compiling this index—69 years after his death, Babe Ruth still has the most entries in this book. But Aaron Judge, who was a rookie in 2017, has more than a dozen entries of his own.

I was surprised at how many times Bill Dickey's name appeared. I know he's a Hall of Famer and had his uniform number (8) retired by the Yankees, but it always seemed to me that like pitcher Waite Hoyt (a native New Yorker and also a Hall of Famer), Dickey has been frequently overlooked as a great Yankee.

TEAMS

Teams that stayed put but changed their names (e.g., Boston Bees/Boston Braves, Los Angeles/California Angels, Tampa Bay Devil Rays/Rays, Florida/Miami Marlins) are listed once. Teams that moved (Boston/Milwaukee/Atlanta Braves, Philadelphia/Kansas City/Oakland Athletics) have separate listings. Teams that moved and changed their names (St. Louis Browns/Baltimore Orioles, Washington Senators/Minnesota Twins, Washington Senators/Texas Rangers, Seattle Pilots/Milwaukee Brewers) also are listed separately.

Arizona Diamondbacks 58, 155, 159, 160, 161

Atlanta Braves 56, 147, 152, 153, 154

Baltimore Orioles 21, 35, 42, 85, 95, 97, 108, 112, 140

Boston Bees/Braves 56

Boston Red Sox 3, 30, 32, 40, 50, 56, 59, 64, 68, 76, 100, 105, 109, 115, 125, 127, 128, 129, 130

Brooklyn Dodgers 24, 114, 118, 126, 133

California/Anaheim/Los Angeles Angels 44, 53, 81, 103, 125

Chicago Cubs 21, 58, 110, 123, 124

Chicago White Sox 43, 44, 67, 87, 108, 119

Cincinnati Reds 137, 151

Cleveland Indians 26, 34, 46, 86, 98, 125, 155

Colorado Rockies 21

Detroit Tigers 9, 42, 49, 51, 59, 60, 62, 73, 74, 89, 91, 101, 102, 103, 104, 123

Houston Astros 23, 56

Kansas City Athletics 1, 44, 125, 165

Kansas City Royals 77, 110, 129, 147

Los Angeles Dodgers 21, 65, 128, 129, 150

Los Angeles Rams 96

Miami/Florida Marlins 21

Milwaukee Braves 134, 135

Milwaukee Brewers 23, 56, 65, 72, 80

Minnesota Twins 21, 25, 29, 43, 106, 119

New York Giants 7, 11, 80, 132, 133, 138, 140, 141, 142, 143, 144

New York Mets 10, 21, 103, 154

Oakland Athletics 44, 53, 83, 90, 110

Philadelphia Athletics 26, 47, 48, 55, 63, 98, 108, 123

Philadelphia Phillies 21, 45, 83, 86, 155, 156, 160

Pittsburgh Pirates 77, 145

San Diego Padres 10, 65, 68, 103

San Francisco Giants 106, 138, 155